A DOSSIER *of* TEXTS RELATING TO GERASIMOS AVLONITES

A DOSSIER *of* TEXTS RELATING TO GERASIMOS AVLONITES

EDITED BY

TED A. CAMPBELL

BRIDWELL PRESS
SOUTHERN METHODIST UNIVERSITY
DALLAS, TEXAS

Bridwell Press is the professional
publishing arm of Bridwell Library
(SMU Libraries and Perkins School of Theology).
Southern Methodist University

SMU Libraries SMU Perkins School of Theology

Design by Alicia Beebe

Printed in the United States of America

ISBN: 978-1-957946-34-4 (paperback)
ISBN: 978-1-957946-35-1 (open access)

TABLE OF CONTENTS

Introduction

GERASIMOS AVLONITES (Γεράσιμος Αυλονητης; in Latin: Erasmus Aulonita; fl. 1752-1773) was a Greek Christian leader who consistently identified himself as the Greek Orthodox Bishop of Arcadia in Crete. A native of Corfu, then dominated by Venice, he worked in Crete during the period of Ottoman domination there. He traveled in Holland (from 1752), England (ca. 1762-1764), Sweden (1768-1769) and Switzerland (1772-1773), leaving a trail of letters and other writings in mixed Greek and Latin in each place. This is an attempt to put together all of the known sources for Gerasimos with transcriptions of manuscript materials and translations of all of the materials.

I have kept – so far as I can discern them – the spellings and accent marks that Gerasimos himself wrote. He was frequently inconsistent in spelling, often substituting other letters or combinations of letters (like the οι diphthong) pronounced like eta (η), and his accents do not conform to contemporary usage.

The translations following the Greek and Latin letters are my own.

I want to thank Christopher Clarke, Research and Instruction Librarian at Bridwell Library (SMU) for his assistance in helping to discern Gerasimos's often confusing and irregular accent marks. I also want to thank Bridwell Library Director Anthony Elia and the Bridwell Library staff for encouraging me to include this volume in a new series from Bridwell Library. I want to thank Elisa McCune, in particular, for her work in securing images of letters and permissions to use those images in addition to her work in formatting this book.

Ted A. Campbell
Albert C. Outler Professor of Wesley Studies
Perkins School of Theology, SMU

1 Gerasimos's Introduction to *Petra tou Skandalou*

1762

Source: Introduction signed by Avlonites in [Elias Meniatis] Πετρα του Σκανδαλου [*Petra tou Skandalou*] ... *i.e. Lapis Offendiculi sive Expositio Originis et Causae Discidis Duarum Orientalis scilicet Occidentalis Ecclesiarum, cum Quinque Controversiis* (London: J. C. Haberkorn, 1762), unnumbered pages following the title pages [2] – [7]. The Greek and Latin versions of the introduction are given on facing pages. The Greek text as printed in this document did not appear in earlier editions of *Petra tou Skandalou* and does not have any accents or breathing marks, perhaps a sign that it was hastily added.

GREEK INTRODUCTION

Ουδεν ουτως Θεω περισπουδαστον ως αγαπη, δια τουτου γαρ ο Θεος εδωκε τον υιον αυτου τω κοσμω και υιος εκεινος Θεανθρωπος μεχρι θανατου υπνος εστι τω πατρι αυτου. δια τουτου γαρ και η πρωτη κλησις των μαθητων αυτου αδελφοι δυο γεγονασιν: ενδεξαμενου δια των προοιμιων ευθυς του πανσοφου Σωτηρος, οτι παντας τους μαθητας αυτου αδελφικως συναπτεσθαι βουλεται. αγαπης τοινυν μηδεν η γωμεθα πρωτιμωτερον, η περ συνδει παντα και εν ομονοια συμφρουση Φυλαττει. Τοιουτοτροπως τω διδασκαλω Χριστω λεγοντι, «εν τουτω γνωσονται παντες οτι εμοι μαθται εστε, εαν αγαπην εχετε εν αλληλοις.»

Επομενος ο Ιερος Ισιδωρος εν ταις αυτου επιστολαις γραφει. τουτου λοιπον του συνδεσμου της ομονοιας και ενοτητος οντος πολυχρονιου εν τη του Χρ[ιστου] καθολικη και αποστολικη εκκλησια, ο σπορευς των ζιζανιων φθονησας διειλε και διεχωρισε, και χασμα μεγα, η μαλλον ειπεν χρισμα μεγα, και την μιαν εις δυο εποιησε. τα πραγματα λογων ου χρηζει, αυτου γαρ εστι Φαινομενα και πασιν υμων δηλα, αλλα προς μειζονα ενδειξιν και σαφεινιαν πασι τας περιεργως και ορθως ζητουσι, δη ην αιτιαν τουτο γεγονε.

Γερασιμος Αυλονητης,
Επισκοπος εν Αρκαδια

LATIN INTRODUCTION

Quod Deo sit magis gratum, quam caritas, omnino nihil est. Hac enim permotus ipse Deus filium suum unigenitum dedit mundo, et filius iste Θεανθρωπος ad mortem vsque obediends Patri suo fuit. Id circo etiam primi, quos vocauit, vt essent eius discipluli, duo fratres fuerant: statim nempe in ipso principio sapientissimus Salvator declarauit, se, vt omnes discipuli sui fraterni amoris vinculo colligentur, velle. Nihil igitur anteponendam caritati ducamus, quippequae omnia connectit, omnia in concordia admodum continet. In hunc modum ipse Doctor Christus asserit: *Ex hoc omnes cognoscent, vos esse discipulos meos, so caritatem inter vos mutuam habueritis.*

Hunc sequutus est Sanctus Isidorus, qui in epistolis suis ita scribit: "Eiusmodi Vinculum concordiae et vnitatis in Catholica atque Apostolica Ecclesia Christi, quum longos per annos duravisset, infelicis Iolii seminator invidens rupit id atque discerpit, magnum hiatum, seu, vt clarius dicam, discidium fecit inter eas, vnamque ante in duas dilacerauit partes." Multis verbis res tam certa, et unicuiquevestru per se notissima non egit: verum maioris demonstrationis certudinisque gratia omnibus curiose, recteque causam discidii huius indagantibus hoc factum est.

Erasmus Aulonita
Episcopus in Arcadia

ENGLISH TRANSLATION

"With God there can be nothing greater than love.[1] For by this God himself sent his only son into the world and this Son was God-man (*theanthropos*),[2] obeying[3] his Father all the way to death.[4] For this reason the first calling of his disciples were two brothers[5] and thus the Most Wise Savior declared even from the beginning point that he wished all of his disciples to be like brothers.[6] Therefore we can place nothing before love, which indeed connects all things together." In the same way Christ our Teacher says, "By this, all know that you are my disciples, if you love one another."[7]

Saint Isidore follows this, who in his letters wrote, "So in this chain of concord and unity in the catholic and apostolic church of Christ, when it had endured through many long years, the one who sows weeds[8] looked upon it with envy, broke and dismembered it, and, if I may speak more clearly, created a huge division between them, so that what was formerly one was ripped into two parts." Many words are not necessary because they are obvious, but the virtue of greater reasons and clarity are offered for all who investigate carefully and justly the cause of this division.

Gerasimos Avlonites[9]
Bishop in Arkadia

1 The letter begins with a quotation from one of the letters of Isidore of Pelusium addressed "To Eusebius the Presbyter" (identified as Book I, Letter 10, in J.-P. Migne, ed., *Patrologiae Cursus Completus: Series Graeca*, 78:185-186, though the Lat. given here does not answer to the Lat. text in the later Migne edition). The word for "love is" Gr. αγαπη (no accents or breathing marks are given in the introduction); Lat. *caritas*.

2 The Lat. text retains the Gr. word Θεανθρωπος.

3 Gr. Υπνος, but Lat. *obedien[d]s*.

4 Philippians 2:8; the Greek phrase translated "to death" (μέχρι θανάτου) reproduces that of the received text of the New Testament; the Latin phrase *ad mortem usque* differs only in word order from the Vulgate *usque ad mortem*. This sentence differs from the text of the letter of Isidore of Pelusium noted above.

5 Matthew 4:18 and ff.

6 Translating the Gr. "brotherly" or "like brothers" (αδελφικως) here; the Lat. has the more expansive, "bound together by a chain of love."

7 John 13:35; the version given here in Latin is not the Vulgate, which has for this verse, *In hoc cognoscent omnes quia mei discipli estis: si dilectionem habueritis ad invicem*. This is consistent with Gerasimos' usage elsewhere in which he gives the Greek (Byzantine) text as the original and offers what is apparently his own Latin translation of the passage.

8 Mat. 13: 24–30, 36–43.

9 Lat. "Erasmus Aulonita, Bishop in Arcadia."

2 Letter of John Richardson to Charles Wesley

March 13, 1764

Source: A ms. copy of the letter in a scrapbook of materials on ordinations in the Methodist Archives, the John Rylands University Library of Manchester, identified as "MAM MA 1977/502". Image provided by The John Rylands Research Institute and Library, The University of Manchester. Material from the Methodist collection deposited at The John Rylands Research Institute and Library is used with the permission of The John Rylands University Librarian and Director of the University of Manchester Library and The Trustees for Methodist Church Purposes (The Methodist Church in Britain).

March 13, 1764
Richards[1] – of Greek Ordination
To the Rev. Mr. Charles Wesley

Dear Sir,
As your brother has now left us, we hope to hear of your speedy coming to us & the rather as there is an affair now in agitation[2] which in my apprehension will be a means of giving our enemies a great advantage against us – namely – Dr Jones's officiating as a Clergyman among us. I have offered him reasons in writing to induce him to forbear acting in that character – exactly the same in substance, and for the most part in expression with those contain'd in the other ***[3] sheet, a Copy of which has been also given to your brother which I was writing to acquaint you with, as I understand there is to be a Conference between you two upon the point.

I remember you were much against Mr Coghlan's ordination by the same & I grant the circumstances between his & Dr Jones's ordination differ, yet I conceive that the substance is the same and that they must both stand or fall together. To clear the matter (as I conceive) it has been plausibly said, that when a popish priest recants his error, he is not re-ordained – I grant it, but believe he cannot legally exercise the office of a priest in the Established Church

1 John Richardson's surname is consistently given as "Richards" in ms. letters and comments like this, though Charles Wesley's endorsement of his letter of 20 January 1765 (below) gives his full surname.
2 The word is scored through though it is necessary for the completion of the sentence.
3 This denotes illegible material, here and later in the letter.

Dear Sir,

As your Brother has now left us, we hope to hear of your speedy coming to us; & the rather as there is an affair now in agitation, which, in my apprehension, will be a means of giving our Enemies a great Advantage against us, namely, Dr. Jones's officiating as a Clergyman among us. I have offered him Reasons in writing to induce him to forbear acting in that Character, — exactly the same in Substance, & for the most part in Expression, — with those contained in the other half Sheet; a Copy of which has been also given to your Brother; which I was willing to acquaint you with, as I understand there is to be a Conference between you two upon the point

I remember you was much set against Mr. Coghlin's Ordination, by the same man; & tho' I grant that the Circumstances between his & Dr. Jones's Ordination differ, yet I conceive that the Substance is the same, & that they must both stand & fall together.

To clear the matter (as I conceive) it has been plausibly said, that when a popish priest recants his Errors, he is not re-ordained; I grant it, but believe he cannot legally ~~act as~~ exercise the office of a priest in the established Church, without the allowance of the Bp. or Arch-bishop. But however that be, the Circumstances between that & the present Case, widely differ. For in the one Case, the man professes popery & subjection to the Church of Rome, & is ordained by a Bishop of that Church; & I believe it is generally abroad. In the other Case, a Greek Bishop (or one supposed to be so) comes into England, & exercises the office of Ordination, not among his own Countrymen nor those of his own Church; but among English people, & those of the established Church, who have no Connexion with or Dependance upon the Greek Church; but on the contrary believe that Church to abound with Errors almost as bad as the papists. And therefore I as much wonder, that any Member of our national Church should submit to receive Orders from a Greek Bishop (let the Suspicion be as much overlooked as possible) as I should, if he was to go to a popish Bishop for Orders, which I suppose would not be submitted to. And I as much wonder that a Greek Bishop of probity & conscientiousness, should ordain any one that he must be persuaded (if he believes the Doctrines of his own Church) holds many & great Errors.

If this Ordination be allowed of, we may expect (if any body else should appear here in the Character of a Greek Bishop) that it will be followed by many others. And can it be supposed that our Bishops will sit still & suffer such a principal part of their Office to be usurped by Foreigners, when even themselves cannot canonically exercise their Office, out of their own Dioceses? It is therefore to be feared, that if this affair be suffered to go on, it will be found that it was the wrongest

Step

Letter of John Richardson to Charles Wesley, March 13, 1764

without the allowance of the Bishop or Archbishop – but however that be, the circumstances between that & the present case widely differ – for in that case the man professes popery & subjection to the church of Rome was ordained by a Bishop of the Church, and, I believe it is generally agreed –In the other case, a Greek bishop (or one supposed to be so), comes into England & exercises the office of Ordination, not among his own Countrymen, or those of his own Church, but among English people & them of the Establish'd Church who have no connexion with, or dependence upon the Greek church, but on the contrary believe that church to abound in errors, about as bad as the popish – and therefore I as much wonder that any member of our national Church should submit to receive orders from a Greek bishop (let the **ption be as uncontroverted as possible) as I should if he was to go to a popish Bishop for orders which I suppose would not be submitted to – and I as much wonder that a Greek Bishop of probity & ***ness should ordain any one that he must be persuaded (if he believes the doctrines of his own Church) held many & great errors – If this ordination be allowed of, we may expect (if any body else should appear here in the character of a Greek Bishop) that it will be allowed by many others & can it be supposed that our Bishops will sit still and suffer such a principal part of their office to be usurped by foreigners, when even themselves cannot canonically exercise their own office out of their own Dioceses – It is therefore to be feared that if this affair be suffered to go on it will be found that it was the wrongeststep that we Methodists ever took & will expose them most to the cause of their enemies – all which is humbly submitted to your serious consideration by,

Dear Sir,
Yours very affectionately,
R. Richards
13 March 1764
To the Rev Mr Charles Wesley

Step that the Methodists ever took, & will expose them most to the Rage of their Enemies.

All which, is humbly submitted to your serious Consideration, by,

Dear Sir,

Yours very affecty,

J Richardson

13th March 1764 —

To the Revd Mr. Chas. Wesley

Letter of John Richardson to Charles Wesley, March 13, 1764

3 John Richardson, "Reasons humbly offered against Dr Jones's officiating as a Clergyman"

March 1764

Source: A ms. copy of the letter in a scrapbook of materials on ordinations in the Methodist Archives, the John Rylands University Library of Manchester, identified as "MAM MA 1977/502", following the previous letter. Image provided by The John Rylands Research Institute and Library, The University of Manchester. Material from the Methodist collection deposited at The John Rylands Research Institute and Library is used with the permission of The John Rylands University Librarian and Director of the University of Manchester Library and The Trustees for Methodist Church Purposes (The Methodist Church in Britain).

Reasons humbly offered against Dr Jones's officiating as a Clergyman

1st Because there were great suspicions last summer touching the character of the person who ordained him – it was questioned whether he was a real Bishop and, if he was, whether he had not left his own country upon account of some issues or misbehaviours – Till these things are fully cleared up to the Satisfaction of the Society (many of whom have entertained the above suspicions and were determined not to receive Mr Coghlan as an ordained Minister) the validity of his orders may justly be suspected.

2ndly But supposing him to be a real Bishop of a Greek Church & that he stands clear of suspicions of any kind, it is clearly [really?] apprehended that he has not according to our laws, & the constitution of our national Church (of which we profess ourselves members) any right or power to exercise his episcopal character here & that no person ordained by him can be acknowledged a minister of the Church of England or (lawfully) use the Office of the Church, & that if any one would do so, he would be liable to a prosecution in the Ecclesiastical Court where his (supposed) Ordination by a foreign Bishop would not be regarded – besides this would be a means & the most effectual means of raising up the Bishops & Clergy against the Methodists, for such a proceeding must needs force them in a tender point & they would undoubtedly use all their power to put a stop thereto – I behoves every one therefore to take care how they become instrumental in doing any thing that way be a means of stirring

Reasons humbly offered against Dr. John Jones's officiating as a Clergyman

1st Because there were great Suspicions last Summer, touching the Character of the Person who ordained him. It was questioned whether he was a real Bishop or not? And if he was, whether he had not left his own Country, upon Account of some Crimes or Misbehaviour? Till these things are fully cleared up to the Satisfaction of the Society (many of whom have entertained the above Suspicions, & were determined not to receive Mr. Coghlan as an ordained Minister) the Validity of his Orders may justly be suspected

2dly But supposing him to be a real Bishop of the Greek Church, & that he stands clear of Suspicions of every kind; It is really apprehended, that he has not, according to our Laws, & the Constitution of our national Church (of which we profess our selves Members) any Right or power to exercise his episcopal Character here; & that no person ordained by him, can be acknowledged as a Minister of the Church of England, or (lawfully) use the Offices of the Church & that if any one should do so, he would be liable to a prosecution in the Ecclesiastical Court, where his (supposed) Ordination by a foreign Bishop, would not be regarded. Besides, this would be a means & the most effectual means of rousing up the Bishops & Clergy against the Methodists. For such a proceeding must needs touch them in a tender point; & they would undoubtedly use all their power to put a Stop thereto. It behoves every one therefore to take Care, how they become instrumental in doing any thing that may be a means of stirring up our Enemies against us, lest they become answerable both to God & Man, for the Consequences

3dly It is humbly apprehended that the Concurrence of Mr. Cha. Wesley should be had in an Affair of so great Consequence. Is he consenting thereto? We look upon the two Brothers to be our joint Ministers, & humbly conceive that nothing of Importance (especially of so great Importance) should be undertaken without their joint Consent. If it be. May it not be productive of Divisions among our selves? It is therefore humbly hoped & desired, that Dr. Jno. Jones may forbear the Exercise of an ordained Minister, till the two Brothers have had a personal Conference upon it & until also, full Satisfaction be given, both as to the Validity of the Ordination it self, & also as to the Legality of it according to our Laws & Constitution; especially as

4thly By the Act of Uniformity. 14th Cha. 2d It is enacted, that no person whatsoever shall presume to consecrate or administer the holy Sacrament of the Lord's Supper, before he be ordained Priest, according to the form & manner prescribed by the Book of Common Prayer, upon pain to forfeit for every offence, the Sum of £100 — It is granted that by the Act of Toleration, Dissenters are exempted from this penalty; but as our above named Brother, is intended to act as a Minister of the Church of England, it will remain in full force against him

It is hoped that these things will be seriously weighed & considered, that

John Richardson, "Reasons humbly offered against Dr Jones's officiating as a Clergyman", March 1764

up our enemies against us lest they become answerable both to God and man for the congregations.

3rdly It is humbly apprehended that the concurrence of one Charles Wesley, would in an affair of so great consequence – to he consenting thereto! –We look upon the two Brothers to be our joint ministers and humbly con*** that nothing of importance (especially of so great importance) should be undertaken without their joint consent – If it be may it not be productive of Divisions among ourselves – it is therefore humbly hoped and denied that Brother Jones may forbear to exercise of an ordained minister till the two brothers have had a personal Conference upon it, & until also full Satisfaction be given, both on the validity of the ordination itself & also as to the legality of it according to our Laws and Constitution, especially as

4thly By the Act of Uniformity 14 Ch 2, it is directed that no person whatever shall presume to consecrate & administer the Holy Sacrament of the Lord's Supper before he be ordained Priest according to the form & manner prescribed by the book of common prayer upon pain to forfeit for every offence the sum of £100 – It is granted that by the act of Toleration Dissenters are exempted from this penalty – but as our above named Brother is intended to act as a Minister of the Ch of Eng it will remain in full force against him.

It is hoped that these things will be seriously weighed & considered that we may act consistently with our profession of members of the Church of England which is to apprehend the introductions [?] of foreign ordinations among us is no sign as [is?] [***] – These are the sentiments of others besides that of an unworthy Brother,

B[rother] Richards[on]
To the Rev Mr John Wesley
A true copy [initials]

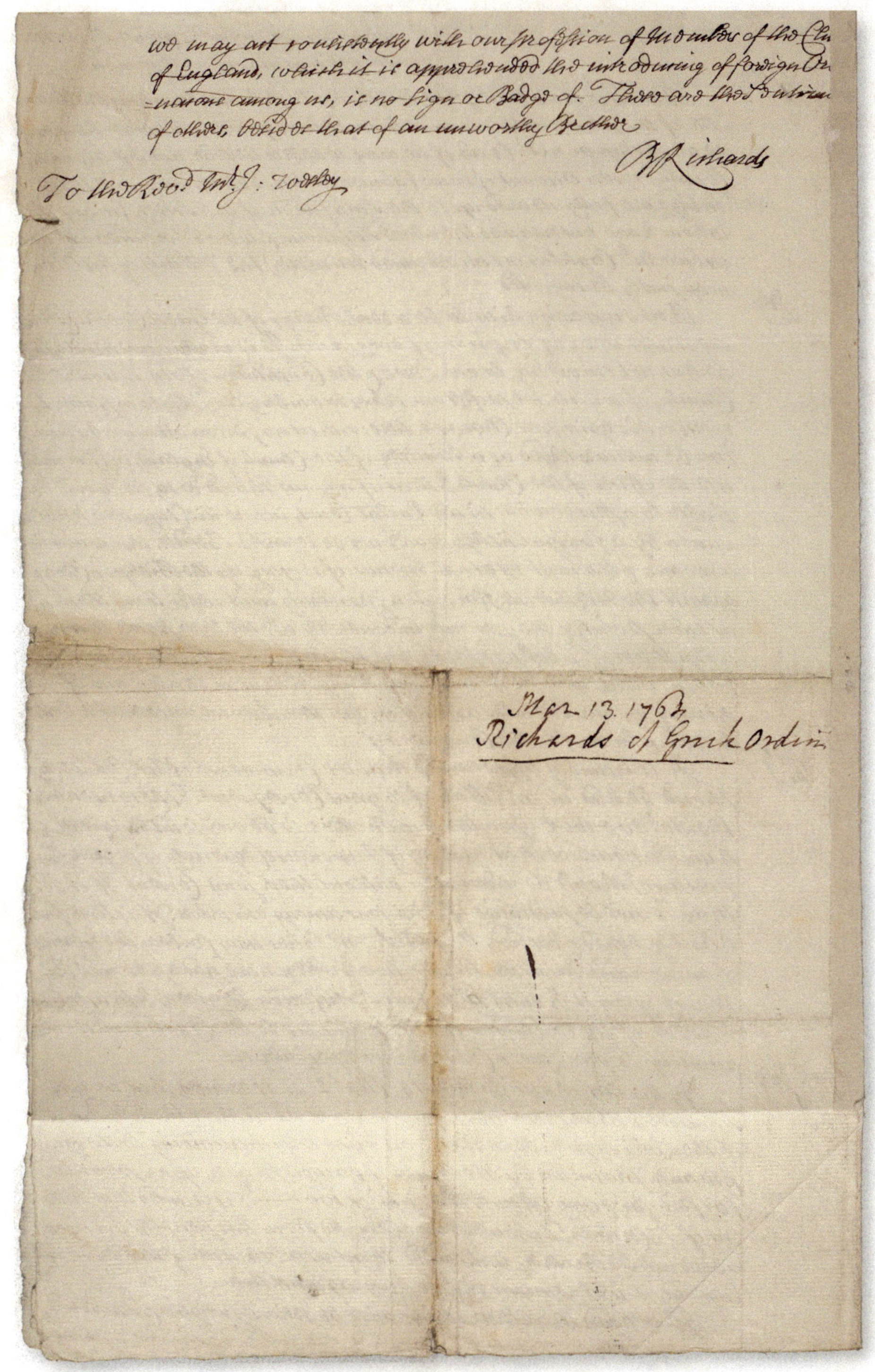
we may act consistently with our profession of Members of the Chu
of England, which it is apprehended the introducing of foreign Or
=nations among us, is no sign or Badge of. These are the Sentim
of others, besides that of an unworthy Brother

B Richards

To the Revd Mr J: [illegible]

Mar 13. 1764
Richards of Greek Ordin

John Richardson, "Reasons humbly offered against Dr Jones's officiating as a Clergyman", March 1764

4 John Newton, Letter to John Wesley

April 24, 1764

Source: A manuscript letter in the United Methodist Archives at Drew University (contact staff for location). Image Courtesy of Special Collections & University Archives, Drew University Library, Madison, New Jersey.

April 24, 1764

John Wesley Esq.

Rev. and Dear Sir

It has been learned lately that there is in Crete a man, the Bishop of Arcadia, who having abundant credentials as to his character has been admitting to the order of deacon, priesthood and the order of bishop by the laying on of hands.

Lady Huntingdon believes his services would be of unestimable value in the creation of a new ministry. Her advise will be in your hands shortly.

John Newton

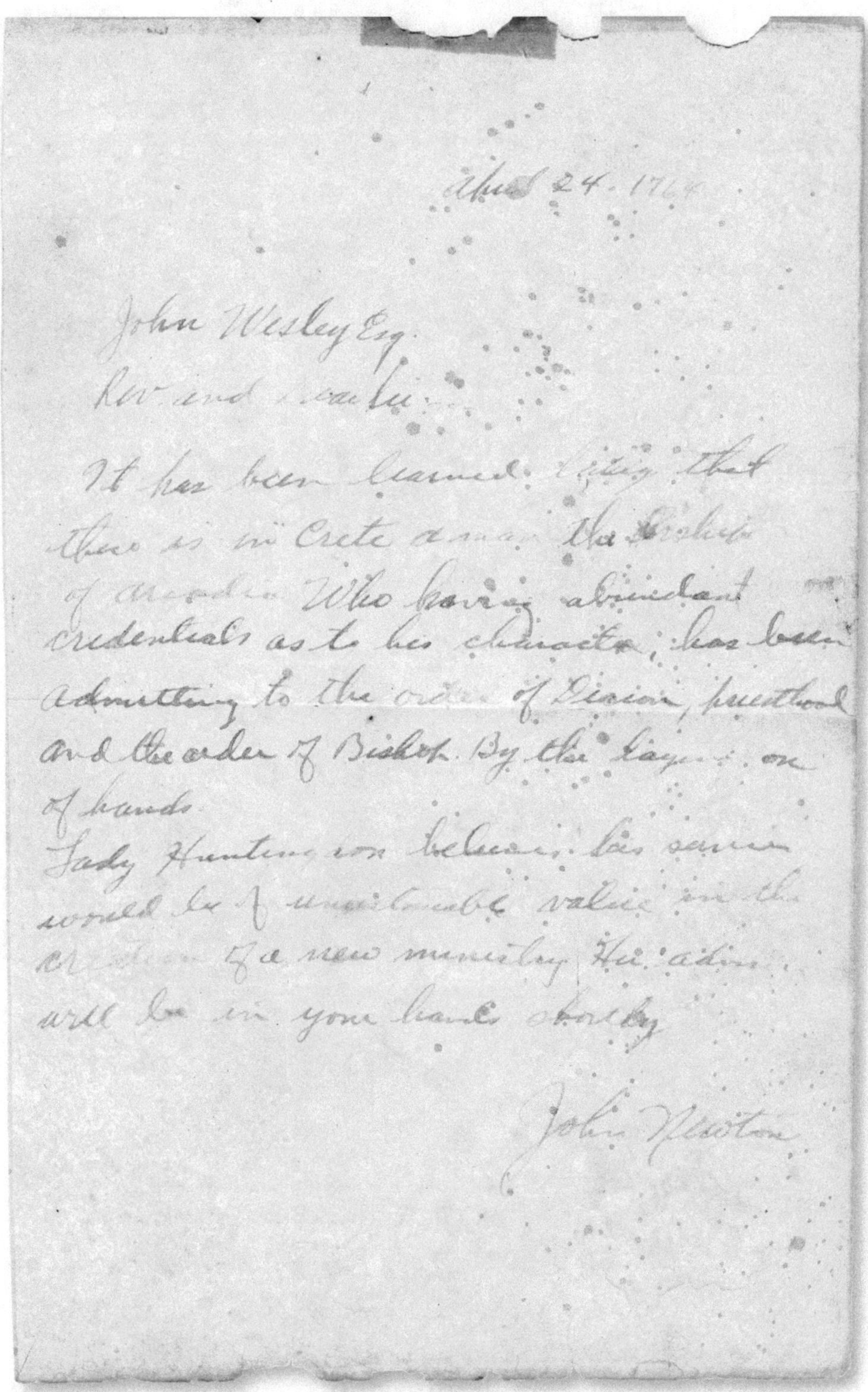

April 24. 1764

John Wesley Esq.
Rev and [illegible]

It has been learned lately that there is in Crete a man the Bishop of Arcadia Who having abundant credentials as to his character, has been admitting to the order of Deacon, priesthood and the order of Bishop. By the laying on of hands.
Lady Huntingdon believes his service would be of unestimable value in the creation of a new ministry. His address will be in your hands shortly

John Newton

John Newton, Letter to John Wesley, April 24, 1764

5 Letter of Gerasimos Avlonites to Charles Wesley

May 30, 1764

Source: a ms. in the John Rylands University Library (JRUL), Manchester, identified as MARC 'DDCW 6/84'. As noted following the transcription, there also exist ms. translations of the letter in the ms. scrapbook held by JRUL as 'MAM MA 1977/502', items 15 and 16. Image provided by The John Rylands Research Institute and Library, The University of Manchester. Material from the Methodist collection deposited at The John Rylands Research Institute and Library is used with the permission of The John Rylands University Librarian and Director of the University of Manchester Library and The Trustees for Methodist Church Purposes (The Methodist Church in Britain).

TRANSCRIPTION

Τῷ αἰδεομωδάτω κυρ[ίῳ] σοΦωδάτω
Κυρίῳ Κυρίῳ Καρόλῳ,
Χαῖρε.

ἀμστερδὰμ αψξδ μαΐου λ

Οἱ πιστέυοντες, οὐ μάχονται πρόστίνας, ἀλλὰ μᾶλλον τοὺς μαχομένους εἰρηνοποίουση, μιμούθομενος τὸν Κύριον. Τοῦτο γὰρ κἀκεῖνος ἐποίησεν ἐχθροὺς ἡμᾶς ὄντας εἰρηνοποίησε πρὸς τον ὁμοούσιον πατέρα. Καὶ πάλιν ὁ πιστέυων, ὀυκ ὀργίζεται, ἀλλὰ μακροθυμεῖ καὶ Φυλάτιει το ὑπὸ τοῦ Κυρίου ῥηθὲν, τὸ μηδ' ολως ὀργίζεσθαι. ὅσα παρακαλῶ τὴν ἡμετέραν ἀγάπην, μὴ μνηοικακῦς, ὀυδὲ ἀποδίδις κακὸν ἀντὶ κακοῦ,[1] ἀλλὰ ἀγάπα τοὺς μισουντάς σε.[2] ὁ προΦήτης Μωϋςῆς εἶπε γὰρ οὕτος πρὸς τὸν λαὸν, ὑμεῖς ἡμαρτήκατε ἁμαρτίαν μεγάλην. Καὶ νῦν ἀναβήσομαι πρὸς τὸν θεὸν οὕτως, ἵνα ἐξιλάσωμαι πρὸς τὸν θεὸν περὶ τῆς ἁμαρτίας ὑμῶν.[3] Καὶ ὁ Δαβὶδ διάθεσιν, διὸ καὶ ἔλεγε, μετὰ τῶν μισούντων τὴν ειρήνην ἥμην εἰρηνικός.[4] ὁρᾶς Σεβασμιώτατε, ὅσαν εἶχον ἀγάπην ὁι ἐν ἀληθείᾳ πιστέυοντες. γινώσκω ὅτι ἡμάρτικα κατά σοὺ, ἀλλὰ ἐγὼ ὀυκ ἐιμὶ ἡ ἀιτία; Τοῦτο Κύριος γινώσκι τοὺς διαλογυσμοὺς τῶν

1 I Thess. 5:15.

2 Cf. Luke 6:27.

3 Exodus 32:30. This and the next passage follow the text of the Septuagint (LXX) exactly except for the doubled phrase "before God" at the end of this verse.

4 Psalm 120:7 (LXX).

Letter of Gerasimos Avlonites to Charles Wesley, May 30, 1764

ἀνθρώπων.[1] οὐδεὶς πιστεύω τὸν ἱερὰν ταύτην πανήγυριν[2] καταισχύνη, τοῦτο ἐστί τὴν ἀγάπην. ἐγὼ πορεύωμενος ἀπὸ ἐνθάδε, καὶ ὁ θεὸς τὸν πατέρον ἡμῶν, τοῦ ἀβραὰμ, και Ἰσαὰκ, και Ἰακὼβ, ἐυλογὴ Φυλάξοι, ἀπὸ πανουργίας ἀνθρώπων πονηρῶν. ἐυοδώση Κύριος τὰς ὁδούς σου, καὶ τὰ ἐντάλματά σου, καὶ ἐν ἐυΦροσύνη εὐφρανθήσεις, καὶ ἐν χαρᾷ διδαχθήσεις καὶ σοὺ, καὶ τοῦ Κυρίου ἀδελΦού σου καὶ Φίλον, καὶ συγγενὸν, ἀυτὸς ὁ θεὸς ἡμῶν, ἐυλογεῖ φυλάξος πάντας ὑπὸ τὴν σκέπην του ἐν εἰρήνη, καὶ ὑποτάξας ὑπὸ τοὺς πόδασας πάντα ἐχθροὺς καὶ πολερμούς. ἔρρωσο.

εἷς ἀθανάτου εὐλάβιας
Γεράσιμος πρωπρ. Ἀρκάδης[3]

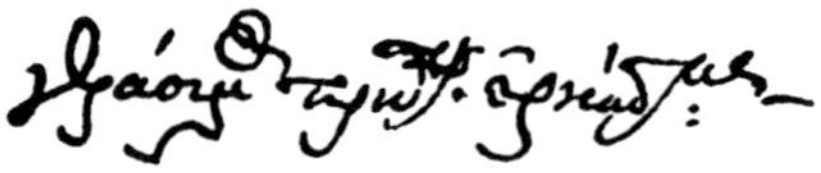

P. S. ὁ καιρὸς εἴγυκε τοῦ πορευθίνε εἰς τὴν ἑλλάδα, θεοῦ θέλοντος, καὶ θεοῦ εὐδοκοῦντος. ὅσα ὁ θεὸς σὲ ἐχάρισι δύναμιν, τράπεζαν πνευματικὴν, καὶ τὴν δόξαν τὴν ἄνω, γένου καὶ ἐυεργέτης. ἀσθενεῖς ἐιμὶ τὴς δυνάμεως περὶ τὴς οδυποριάς μου; μὴ παρωξύνασε ἄφες ἀυτῶ τὴν ὀργὴν. ἡ πενία μου ὀυ ἐμπόδιον γύνετε, ἀλλὰ μάλιστα το μέγεθός ἐστι τῆς ἀρετῆς. παρακαλῶ ἐπέδειξε προαίρεσιν ὀρθὴν ἐλεημοσύνη ἀνδρὸς ὃς σφραγὶς μετ' αυτόῦ. καλλώπισον ἀιδεομώδατε τὴν χεῖρα σου, ἐλεημοσύνη, Φιλανθρωπία, ἀγάπη, ἀπειδὴ ταῦτα τῆς ἀρετῆς τὰ χρώματα. διὰ τοῦτων ἀγγέλους ὀυκ ἀνθρώπους ἐραστὰς ἐπισκᾶ σε. διὰ τὴς ἐλεημοσύνης τὸν θεὸν ἐξεὶς ἐπαινέτω. ἑπτὰ χρόνους κυνδυνεύῳ καὶ νῦν ἐυρὸ καιρὸν ἵνα πορευθῶ. σπλαγχνίσου, τὴν ἐμεὶ ταλεπωρίαν καθὸς θέλεις καὶ οὔγλεσα [σύγλεσα?], ὀυ κατὰ χάριν, ἀλλὰ κατ' δύναμιν. σὺ ἔχεις ἀρετὰς σωφρυσύνην, ἀνδρείαν, Δικαιοσύνην, φρόνησυν, καὶ Φιλανθρωπί[αν,] καὶ διά τοῦτο ἐλπίζω, ἵνα γένης θεαρεστος. μημήσου τὸν ἀβραὰμ τον Φιλόξενον, Ἰὼβ τὸν δύκαιον, τὸν τωβὶτ, τοὺς ἄρτους ἀυτοῦ εὔιδε τοῖς πεινῶσι, καὶ τα ἱμάτια τοῖς γυμνοῖς. λουκᾶς λέγει, πωλήσατε τὰ ὑπάρχοντα ὑμῶν, καὶ δότε πτωχοίς.

1 The word translated "thoughts" (διαλογυσμοὺς) is the same used in Luke 5:22.

2 The same term used at Hebrews 12:22.

3 The first two letters of the name Γεράσιμος employ a common ligature for gamma and epsilon. Later letters (see below) drop the letter gamma in this name. The signature here (see the reproduction of it) does not use the title bishop (ἐπίσκοπος) but instead has 'πρωπρ.' which I take to be an abbreviation for πρωτοπρεσβύτερος.

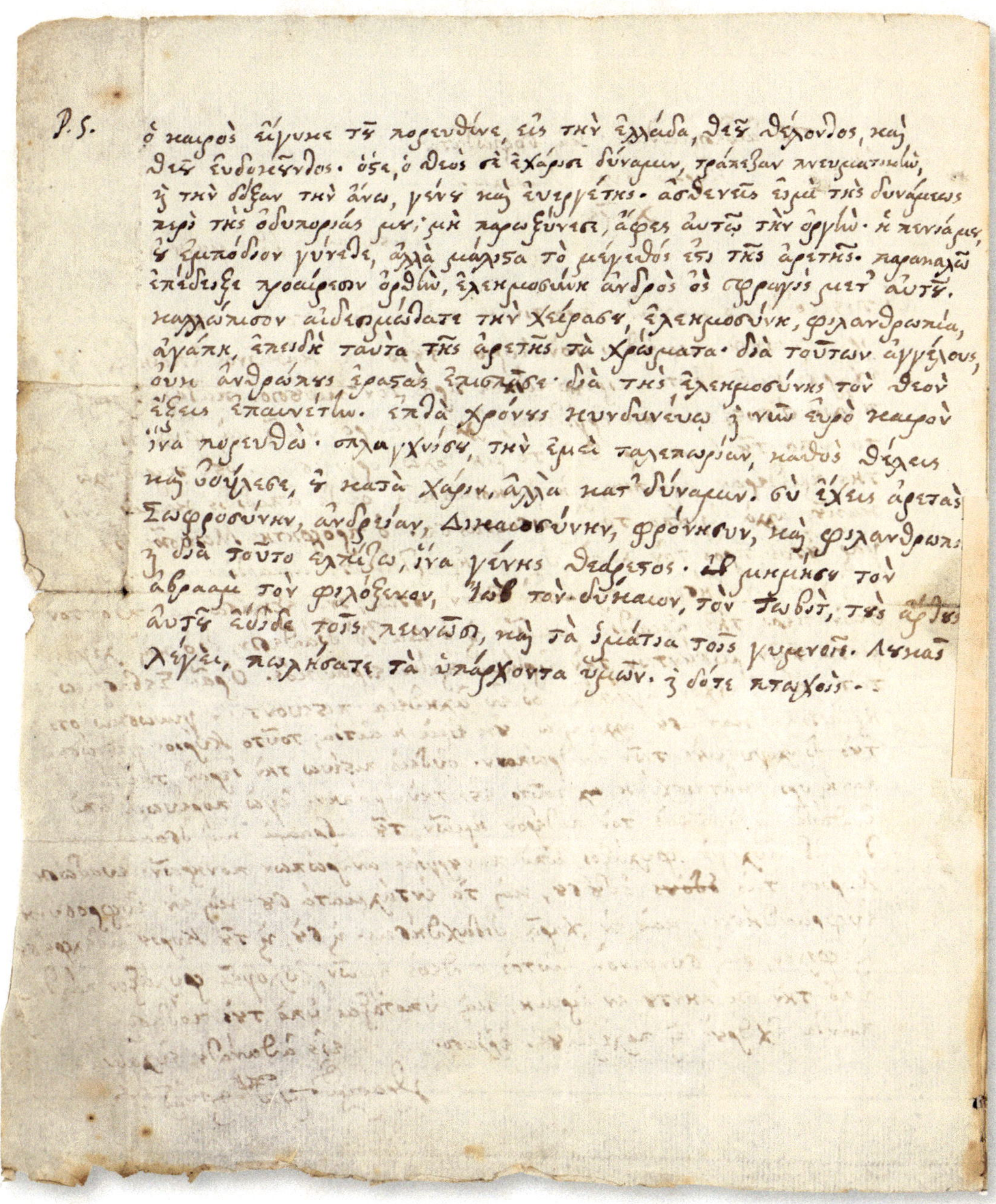

P.S. ὁ καιρὸς ἤγγικε τοῦ πορευθῆναι εἰς τὴν Ἑλλάδα, θεοῦ θέλοντος, καὶ
θεοῦ εὐδοκοῦντος. ὅσα, ὁ θεὸς σοι ἐχάρισε δύναμιν, τράπεζαν πνευματικὴν,
καὶ τὴν δόξαν τὴν ἄνω, γένου καὶ εὐεργέτης. ἀσθενὴς εἰμὶ τῆς δυνάμεως
περὶ τῆς ὁδοιπορίας μου, μὴ παροξύνεσαι, ἄφες αὐτῷ τὴν ὀργὴν. ἡ πενία μου,
οὐ ἐμπόδιον γίνεται, ἀλλὰ μάλιστα τὸ μέγεθος ἐστὶ τῆς ἀρετῆς. παρακαλῶ
ἐπίδειξε προαίρεσιν ὀρθὴν, ἐλεημοσύνη ἀνδρὸς ὡς σφραγὶς μετ᾽ αὐτοῦ.
καλλώπισον αἰδεσιμώτατε τὴν χεῖρά σου, ἐλεημοσύνη, φιλανθρωπία,
ἀγάπη, ἐπειδὴ ταῦτα τῆς ἀρετῆς τὰ χρώματα. διὰ τούτων ἀγγέλους,
οὐκ ἀνθρώπους ἐραστὰς ἐποίησε. διὰ τῆς ἐλεημοσύνης τὸν θεὸν
ἕξεις ἐπαινέτην. ἑπτὰ χρόνους κινδυνεύω, καὶ νῦν εὗρον καιρὸν
ἵνα πορευθῶ. σπλαγχνίσου τὴν ἐμὴν ταλαιπωρίαν, καθὼς θέλεις
καὶ βούλεσαι, οὐ κατὰ χάριν, ἀλλὰ κατὰ δύναμιν. σὺ ἔχεις ἀρετὰς
Σωφροσύνην, ἀνδρείαν, Δικαιοσύνην, φρόνησιν, καὶ φιλανθρωπ[ίαν]
καὶ διὰ τοῦτο ἐλπίζω, ἵνα γένῃς θεόφρετος. μιμήσου τὸν
Ἀβραὰμ τὸν φιλόξενον, Ἰὼβ τὸν δίκαιον, τὸν Τωβίτ, τοὺς ἄρτους
αὐτοῦ ἐδίδου τοῖς πεινῶσι, καὶ τὰ ἱμάτια τοῖς γυμνοῖς. Λουκᾶς
λέγει, πωλήσατε τὰ ὑπάρχοντα ὑμῶν. καὶ δότε πτωχοῖς.

Letter of Gerasimos Avlonites to Charles Wesley, May 30, 1764

TRANSLATION

To the Most Esteemed and Most Wise,
Honorable[1] Charles,
Greeting!

Amsterdam 1764 May 30

Believers do not quarrel with anyone but rather they make peace with those who are quarreling, following the Lord. For he did this: he made us, when we were sinners, to be reconciled to the consubstantial Father.[2] And again, a believer does not grow angry, but has patience and follows the word from the Lord, never to be angry. Thus I ask for the same love: do not bear a grudge, nor return evil for evil,[3] but love those who hate you.[4] For the Prophet Moses spoke in this way to the people, "You have sinned a great sin; and now I will go up to God, that I may make atonement before God for your sin."[5] And David [understood and?] said, "I was for peace among them that hated peace."[6]

You see, most Reverend, what love they have who in truth believe. I know that I have offended you, but it is not my fault. The Lord knows the thoughts of humans.[7] I do not at all believe this sacred festal gathering[8] to have been anything shameful, but rather a love feast.[9]

I am going away from here. May the Father, the God of Abraham, of Isaac, and of Jacob, keep you safe from the deceits of humans. May the Lord guard your paths, and your teachings, rejoicing in knowledge, learning with joy; may our God himself keep in his protection in peace your brother and your relations, and may he put all of your enemies and all your conflicts below your feet. Be strong!

Unto the Praises of the Immortal,
Gerasimos Protopresbyter of Arkadi

1 The Greek expression here (Κυρίῳ Κυρίῳ, lit. "Lord Lord") is used frequently in letters denoting deference to a high official.

2 Cf. Romans 5:10. The term "consubstantial" (ὁμοούσιον) is that used in the Nicene Creed.

3 I Thess. 5:15.

4 Cf. Luke 6:27.

5 Exodus 32:30. This and the next passage follow the text of the Septuagint (LXX) exactly except for the doubled phrase "before God" at the end of this verse.

6 Psalm 120:7 (LXX).

7 The word translated "thoughts" (διαλογυσμοὺς) is the same used in Luke 5:22.

8 The same word used for a 'festal gathering' (πανήγυριν) in Hebrews 12:22. Gerasimos refers here to the assembly in which he ordained some of the Evangelical preachers.

9 ἀγάπην; or perhaps, "an act of great love" in contrast to καταισχύνη, "an act of shame."

[...] Bishop 1762

Wd Peter's zeal ever sold
His heav'nly powers for perishable gold?
At Mamon's beck dispens'd the holy fire,
And made apostles for a Wizard's hire?

What may be the Wizard's hire, I know not: but this I know, — "there is neither "Sense, Connection, or Grammar "either in the Letter or Postscript" however, they carry self-evident Marks, that they were both wrote by one & the same Masterly hand.

To
The Revend. Carolo Wesley
at the Foundery near
Moorfields
London

Letter of Gerasimos Avlonites to Charles Wesley, May 30, 1764

P. S. The time is coming for me to depart for Greece, God willing and God being pleased. May God grant power, spiritual food, the glory from above, to my kinsman and benefactor. I am weak in strength through my suffering; may he not stir up his wrath against him. My poverty has not been an impediment for me, but is the greatest height of virtue. I beg you to show appropriate mercy to the man who is with you. Adorn your most respected hand with mercy, philanthropy, love; fix your eyes on these varieties of virtue. For this reason, may angels, not human friends, lead you. For this mercy you have, praise God. I have attempted seven times and now I find a time when I can depart. Have mercy upon my distress as you please and wish, not according to your will but according to your power. You have the virtues of moderation, manliness, understanding, mindfulness, and philanthropy, and for this reason I hope you will be just. Remember Abraham the friend of strangers, Job the righteous, and Tobit, the food they gave to the poor, and clothing to the naked. Luke says, sell your possessions and give [them] to the poor.[1]

Further information: The ms. letter is addressed 'To / The Revend° Carolo Wesley / at the Foundery near / Moorfields / London'. The letter has the endorsement, '[illegible] Bishop 1764' then the following verses:

– – Wd Peter's zeal heor sold
His hievenly powers for perishable gold?
At Mamon's beck dispensd ethereal fire
And made apostles for a Wizard's hire?[2]

The endorsement continues in the same hand, 'What may be the *Wizard's hire*, I know not: but this I know, – "there is neither *sense*, *connection*, or *grammar* either in the Letter or Post-script"; however, they carry self-evident marks, that they were both wrote by one and the same masterly hand.'

There are two ms. translations of the letter in different hands in the ms. scrapbook 'MAM MA 1977/502' in the John Rylands University Library in Manchester. Item 15 of

1 Luke 18:22.

2 From a poem attributed to Samuel Wesley, the older brother of John and Charles Wesley; in the introduction (by F. R. Raines) to Francis Gastrell, *Notitia Cestriensis: Or, Historic Notices of the Diocese of Chester* (Lancashire: The Chetham Society, 1850), vol. II, part II, p. xlvii.

this scrapbook has a translation in pencil and includes only part of the postscript; item 16 actually has two translations in parallel columns, and includes the entirety of the postscript.

6 Gerasimos Avlonites, Letter Testifying to Ordination of W.C.

November 24, 1764

Source: A translation of the certificate given in Augustus Toplady's Works (6 vols.; London: 1794) 5:346; also in Southey's *Life of Wesley* (London and New York: Frederick Warne and Co., 1889), p. 454, in the footnote.

Our measure from the grace, gift, and power of the all-holy and life-giving Spirit, given by our Saviour Jesus Christ to His divine and holy apostles, [is] to ordain sub-deacons and deacons, and also to advance to the dignity of a priest! Of this grace, which hath descended to our humility, I have ordained sub-deacon and deacon, at Snow Fields Chapel, on the 19th day of November 1764, and at West Street Chapel, on the 24th of the same month, priest, the Rev. Mr. W.C., according to the rules of the holy apostles and of our faith. Moreover, I have given him power to minister and teach, in all the world, the gospel of Jesus Christ, no one forbidding him in the Church of God. Wherefore for that very purpose, I have made this present letter of recommendation from our humility, and have given it to the ordained Mr. W.C.[1] for his certificate and security. – Given and written at London, in Britain, Nov. 24, 1764. / Erasmus, Bishop of Arcadia

1 Possibly William Crabb.

7 Letter of James Thwaytes to Charles Wesley

January 5, 1765.

Source: A ms. letter in the John Rylands University Library of Manchester in a scrapbook of materials related to ordinations identified as MAM MA 1977/502, leaf 19. Image provided by The John Rylands Research Institute and Library, The University of Manchester. Material from the Methodist collection deposited at The John Rylands Research Institute and Library is used with the permission of The John Rylands University Librarian and Director of the University of Manchester Library and The Trustees for Methodist Church Purposes (The Methodist Church in Britain).

In other cases (such as the letters of John Richardson below), I have regularized spelling and filled out abbreviations, but Thwaytes's letter has such an abundance of eccentric spellings (and grammar) that it deserves to be seen in something like its original form.

Revd and Dear Sir –

London Jan. 5th 1764[2]

As you will be apprised by this poast of sumthing which will displeas you I take the freedom to acquaint you my selfe that hath feell oute with oute my seekin or even Desire but a person came to me injoyned me to keep a secret for a tim & then it wass propounded to & I was withoute any Desire perswaded into ordination by the Greek bishope with severall others traveling *** which hath made sum stirr among us hear as Mr Jones hath sett the example & admitted by your Brothers approbation why should we be turnd oute of the Methodist Society for the same falt overlooked in others & blessed be God no one could say any thing to ower Charge since wee was admitted in to your Sosiatey & you canot say so of all that is ordaind & *** this ordenation if Mr Jones will give up his wee are willin to give up owers – –

Dear Sir[3] Excuse my writing to you & pardon me in this thing I remain your sonn in the Gospel, Jas. Thwaites

Further Information: Charles Wesley's endorsement of the letter is as follows: "Thwait Cnfess / Jan 6, 1765". The letter has a part of a red seal and the date stamp "5/IA", i.e., 5 January.

2 1764 in the Old Style calendar that had been introduced eight years earlier. Charles Wesley's endorsement (see the text below) places the letter in January 1765, utilizing the New Style date.

3 This postscript is written vertically in the left-hand margin of the ms.

8 John Richardson, Letter to Charles Wesley

January 20, 1765

Source: A letter in the Methodist Archives, the John Rylands University Library of Manchester, in a scrapbook of materials related to ordinations identified as "MAM MA 1977/502," leaf 9. Image provided by The John Rylands Research Institute and Library, The University of Manchester. Material from the Methodist collection deposited at The John Rylands Research Institute and Library is used with the permission of The John Rylands University Librarian and Director of the University of Manchester Library and The Trustees for Methodist Church Purposes (The Methodist Church in Britain).

Reverend and Dear Sir,

It fama per urbes![1] Bristol I perceive has heard of the madness of our prophets. I wanted to give you a short narrative, but thought some other would do it, that knew more of the secret. Mr. W. has been not a little bowed down. They sing on all sides that he offered a premium to fetch two foreign bishops to help Erasmus (by JJ.[2]) whether he could consecrate him. When it could not be done without more Erasmites, it was dropped. All the rest I suppose is *purum putrem*.[3] On Monday after the last ordination got air, the priests were all cut off at a meeting of stewards and preachers. A formal paper was sent to all them dealing with our names at length. It was unlucky for JJ. that his was there, for J. Th.[4] fell upon him that night at Wapping after he done preaching with, "What a *villain* are you (*bona verba ex puro corde*!)[5] to sit in judgment on me, and are in the same fault!" The Doctor took it all patiently. Brother Thwaytes was at first near to distraction. He has been several times here to worry Mr W. but he has not seen him yet. The grief Mrs Thwaytes had on this account threw her into fits at the Chapel. She is still much burdened and behaves quite well under it. Thwaytes pretends to have letters from several traveling preachers. "Is the Bishop in London? If not tell us where he is in Holland and we will go over." He half threatens to let him loose upon us. "Would it not be

1 "Thus the report goes through the cities"; Virgil, *Aeneid*, 4:173; cf. H. Rushton Fairclough, ed. and tr., *Virgil: Eclogues, Georgics, Aeneid I-VI* (rev. G. P. Gould; Cambridge, Massachusetts, and London: Harvard University Press, 1999), pp. 434-435.

2 John Jones.

3 "Pure rot."

4 James Thwaytes.

5 "Good words from a pure heart."

Revd. & dear Sir.
It fama per urbes! Bristol I perceive has heard of the
madn: of our prophets. I wanted to give you a short Narra-
-tive, but tho't some other wou'd do it, that knew more
of the Secret — Mr. W. has been not a little bowed down. They ring
it on all sides, that he offered a premium to fetch 2 foreign
Bps to help Erasm: to consecrate him Bp. This sprung from his
askg. Eras: (by D.J.) whether he cd. consecrate him — when it cd.
not be done witht. more Erasmites, it was drop'd, All ye rest
I suppose is purum putum — On Monday after ye last Ordinn.
got Air. the priests wre all cut off at a Meetg. of Stewds: & preachrs
A formal paper was sent to all ye Delingts. wth our Names at
length. It was unlucky eno' for D.J. yt his was there: For J. Th:
fell upon him that Night at WPPG after he done preachg with
"wt a villain are you (bona verba ex puro corde!) to sit in
Judgt. on me, & are in ye same fault." The Doct: took it all pa-
:tiently — B. Thw: was at first near to distract — He has been
several times here to worry Mr. W. but he has not seen him
yet — The Grief Mrs. Thw: had on this Acct. threw her into
Fits at the Chap: She is still much burd. & behaves quite
well under it — Thw: pretends to have letters from several
travellg. preachrs "Is the Bp in Lond.? if not tell us where
he is in Holld. & we will go over". He ½ threatens to
let him loose upon us. "Wou'd it not be right consi-
:dering how ill I am used?" He talk'd loudly of going
to Mr. M. but for his Wife's sake stands still at present.

John Richardson, Letter to Charles Wesley, January 20, 1765

right considering how ill I am used?" He talked loudly of going to Mr M.[1] but for his wife's sake stands still at present. John Oliver had passed his word to preach for T. M.[2] yesterday. Notice was given for him. He has since that seen Mr W. and got leave to go hide himself awhile at Colchester. He broke his word with T. M. for *Conscience'* sake. He was afraid of losing the life of God, although they offered him to preach anon! We expect every day to hear of Thomas Bryant's tearing the flock at Sheffield, and setting up for himself. Lackless a local preacher is joined his *Brother* L. Coughlan. Berry & the broker carry no collars yet!

The thoughts of many hearts were revealed at the Covenant in light of T.M. One of his people asked Mr W., "Have you any objection to Mr M. helping you tonight?" "No." So he came! This is your Brother's account to the society last night. He added that he should never come back without confessing his fault at least to all the preachers and stewards in London. This gave much brightness to many faces. I went to T. Butts as you desired, he will be glad to hear from you when it suits. When Mr W. had done in the desk on the Covenant night, he sent for me to give out an hymn in the desk. When I had done, J.J. & T.M. were with him at the altar. He sent for me; I was going till I saw T.M. between Mr W. & JJ. I then stopped and said I *would* not go. I heard no more about it. I wonder they should send particularly for me. Mr W. knew I shunned officiating with JJ. one Tuesday at the Chapel.

As to Mr C. & []y[3] had both laboured with J.J. and I believe [][4] no objections had they been called to minister with T.M. and him that night.

Mr Blackwell has it from some Great Man that the Lords-Spiritual are currently taking some measures to *put an end* to travelling preachers. We are to have a day of humiliation on this account.

Of the blacksiders no more – I think there *is enough to bid you* come and help. After all, I remark in general, the people are much alive, many speak of giving themselves *altogether* to God. As to myself I see no other way to get rest. I have oft-times a multitude of peace, I see the promises as a wall of fire around me ever since you preached on that scripture at the Chapel. But O what wrath I sometimes groan under!

I have no hopes *of getting to Bristol* now, for I have no money to signify, However, if you would fix your time of coming here, I would stretch a point

1 Apparently Thomas Maxfield; see the reference to "T.M." immediately following.

2 Maxfield.

3 The ms. has been taped over at this point.

4 Tape also obscures this area of the ms.

John Oliver had passed his word to preach for T.M. yesterday.
Notice was given for him. He has since that seen Mr. W. & got
leave to go hide himself awhile abt. Colchestr. He broke
his Word wth. T.M. for Conscience' sake. He was affraid of
losing the life of God, altho' they offered him 40£ pr Ann!
We expect evry day to hear of Tho: Bryant's leaving the
Flock at Sheffield, & setting up for himself. Tackless
a local-preacher is joined his Bro: L. Cough: – Berry
& the Broker carry no Colours yet!
The Thots of many hearts were revealed at the Covent.
on sight of T.M. One of his peop: asked Mr. W "have you
any Objection to Mr. M. helpg. you to Night?" "No". So he
came! this is yr. Bro: Acct. to ye. Society last Night. He
added yt. he shd. never come back witht. confessg. his
Fault at least to all the preachers & Stewards in Lond:
This gave much Brightness to many Faces. I
went to T. Butts as you desired, he will be glad to
hear from you when it suits. When Mr. W. had
done in ye. Desk on ye. Covt. Night, he sent for me to
give out an Hymn in ye. Desk. When I had done
J.J. & T.M. were wth. him at ye. Altar. He sent for me:
I was going, till I saw, T.M. betw: Mr. W. & J.J. I then
stopped & said I woud not go. I heard no more about
it. I wonder they shd. send particly. for me. Mr. W.
knew I shun'd officiatg. wth. J.J. one Tuesd: at ye. Chap:

John Richardson, Letter to Charles Wesley, January 20, 1765

> and come *a fortnight* before to bring you up. My health is a little better. My kind love to Mrs Wesley and *my play*-fellows, James Pearce and his sister concludes me, Dear Sir, your ever obliged servant in it,
>
> JR
>
> [P.S.] I beg your prayers. I gain much more by the prayers of others than I do by my own.

Further Information: The ms. letter is addressed, "To / The Revd Mr Chas: Wesley / in / Bristol". Charles Wesley's endorsement of the letter is as follows: "Jan. 20, 1765 / B. Richardson / History of the / Priests & T.M." The letter carries an indication of four pence postage paid and has the date stamp "21/IA" i.e., 21 January.

As to Mr. C. & J[illegible] [illegible]y had both laboured wth.
J.J. & I believe [illegible] no Objectns. had they been
called to minister wth. T. M. & him that night.

Mr. Blackwell has it from some Great Man
that the Lords-Spiritual are certd. takg. some Measures
to put an End to travellg. preachg— We are to have a
Day of Humiln. on ye Acct—

Of the black side no more—
I think there is enough to bid you come & help— after
all, I remark in general, the peop: are much alive, many
speak of Giving themselves altogr. to God. As to myself
I see no other way to get rest— I have oft-times a Multit.
of Peace, I see ye promises as a wall of Fire around me
ever since you preachd on that Scripture at ye. Chappl
But O wt. wrath I somets. groan under!
I have no hopes of gettg. to Brist: now, for I have no Money
to signify. Howevr. if you wd. fix yr. time of comg. here, I wd.
stretch a point & come a fortnight before to bring you
up— my health is a little better. My kind love to
Mrs. Wesley & my play-fellows, Sar: pearce & her Sister
concludes me, Dear Sir, Yr. ever obliged Servt. in X.

J.R.

I beg yr. prayr: I gain more by ye prayers of others
than I do by my own—

John Richardson, Letter to Charles Wesley, January 20, 1765

9 Anonymous Letter to the *St James's Chronicle*

February 6, 1765

Source: An anonymous letter published in the *St James's Chronicle* (Feb. 7–9, 1765), 4.

Sir,

The Letter in your Paper of the 12th, dated from Oxford, signed A. P. and another from the same Gentleman before, dated I think, from Newington; likewise those Queries, signed J. T. in your Paper of the 31st of January last, with all those Hints in the publick Papers, relative to the Ordination by the Greek Bishop, I believe to be the produce of Mr. W – y, or his Dependents l'ens, because no other could know so well the State of the Affair concerning the Greek Bishop and those ordained: But what is all this for? If by any means to stir up the Minds of the People and Clergy against them, because these people will not submit to his Tyranny any longer. Oh! this Smithfield Work; real Christians would have no hand in it, but let each Man answer to his own Master. Blessed be God we have upright Men in the Courts at Westminster.

Those queries are so drawn up so as to fall directly into his fallacious Net, on which to clear himself, he, doubtless, will fix a Negative; but in order to guard the Unwary from being led away by any Fallacy, knowing the Truth, I will answer it, as far as I can, with Matters of Fact.

"Were Mr. W – y's preachers ordained by his knowledge?" Mr. J. J – s was, for he himself was at the Head of his Ordination, from which all the others sprung. "Will he receive them as Clergymen?" He doth Mr. J. J – s, who hath acted in that Function some Time under him, and consequently thinks the Ordination valid, or he would not have desired Consecration himself from the Bishop; who told me himself that Mr. J. W – y had desired Mr. J – s to know of him, if he would consecrate him Bishop, and received for Answer, that in the Greek Church no Priest could be consecrated Bishop, unless in the Presence of three Bishops of that Church: But the Bishop refused it, which shewed him honest. With this agreed the Testimony of Mr. J – s to Mr. S – n of Deptford, who was enquiring what Mr. W – y thought of the Validity of the Greek Bishop's Ordination: Answered he, Mr. W – y thought it valid, for he would have been consecrated Bishop himself by him if he could.

But this huge Cry of poor unlearned Men being ordained, put me on the Enquiry who were objects according to the written Word; and I found none were chosen because they understood Logick, Rhetorick, or Philosophy, but those who had received that Wisdom from above, to teach them what they were by Nature and actual Transgression, that there was sufficient Strength laid on One mighty to save, who lay hold on him by Faith, and through it find Peace with God, and bring forth the Fruits of the Spirit, in their Lives and Conversation. What have Logick, Philosophy, or the Eastern Languages to do with this? Hath not God chose the foolish Things of this world to confound the Wise? He took Elisha from the Plough, and the Apostles from their Fishing-Nets, to make them Fishers of Men; and will Men call these the Dregs of the People, whom God hath thus sent forth?

A few of those meet a Bishop, Successor of that very Church St. Paul ordained Titus into – Crete: He, looking on them as Objects the Ministry, laid Hands on them; ordaining them to that Ministry which the Holy Ghost had before established them in. "But he is from turkey, therefore can have no Power in England." St. Paul, who ordained his Predecessor, I suppose did not mind whether he was in Asia, or Europe; but where he found proper Objects, he administered the Ordinance. "But he read the Ceremony in Greek, and they did not understand it," What then? Suppose there had not been a Word spoken, more than was spoke to Elisha on the same Occasion of old; they came there to ordain and be ordained; this they knew, and appeared before God; the Bishop laid his Hand on them for that Purpose. Yet there was an Interpreter. "But Money should not be given." Yes, what he had; for his Exigences only: He had no more. "But ought not Clergymen to be Men of Learning, to answer the Gainsaying of Infidels?" God hath never failed to raise up a Paul in every Age; when he saw it requisite.

Oh, when will this Bitterness of Spirit be banished from those who profess Christianity!

February 6, 1765

10 John Wesley, Letter to the Printer of the *St James's Chronicle*

February 5, 1765

Source: A letter published in the *St James's Chronicle* (Feb. 7–9, 1765), 4; cf. John Telford, ed., *Letters of the Rev. John Wesley, A.M.* ("Standard Edition" of the Works of John Wesley; 8 vols.; London: Epworth Press, 1931), 4:288-9.

[London,
February 5, 1765][1]

Sir,

To the four Questions proposed to me in your last Week's Paper, I answer:

1. None of those six Persons lately ordained by a Greek Bishop were ordained with my Consent or Knowledge.
2. I will not, cannot own or receive them as Clergymen.
3. I think an Ordination performed in a Language not understood by the Persons ordained, is not valid.
4. I think it is absolutely unlawful for any one to give Money to the Bishop (or to any one for him) for ordaining him.

I
am, Sir,
your humble servant,

John Wesley

1 The date and place are supplied from the time of publication Wesley's itinerary in this period.

11 Excerpt from John Wesley, Letter to the Printer of the *St James's Chronicle*

February 10, 1765

Source: A letter published in the *St. James's Chronicle* (Feb. 12–14, 1765), 4; cf. Telford, ed., *Letters*, 4:289-90.

Sir,

In the St. James's Chronicle, published on Saturday last, there was an innocent Thing wrote by a Hat-Maker in Southwark. It may be proper to take a little more Notice of it than it deserves, lest Silence should appear to be an acknowledgement of the Charge.

I insert nothing in the public Papers without my Name. I know not the Authors of what has been lately inserted; Part of which I have not seen y[e]t, nor did I see any Part before it was printed.

A Year or two ago I found a Stranger perishing for Want and expecting daily to be thrown in Prison. He told me he was a *Greek* Bishop. I examined his Credentials, and was fully satisfied. After much Conversation (in Latin and Greek, for he spoke no English at all) I determined to relieve him effectually, which I did without Delay, and promised to send him back to Amsterdam, where he had several Friends of his own Nation. And this I did without any farther View, merely upon Motives of Humanity. After this he ordained Mr. John J. a Man well versed both in the Languages and other Parts of Learning.

When I was gone out of town, Bishop Earasmus [*sic*] was prevailed upon to ordain L – C – , a person who had no Learning at all.

Some Time after, Mr. M – d, or his Friends, sent for him from Amsterdam, to ordain Mr. S – t[2] and three other Persons, *as unlearned* as any of the Apostles; but I believe not *so much inspired*.

In December last he was sent for again, and ordained six other Persons, members of our society, but every Way, I think, unqualified for that Office. These I judged it my Duty to disclaim (to waive all other Considerations) for a

2 Unidentified.

Fault which I know not who can excuse, *buying* an Ordination in an *unknown Tongue*.

As to the other tale, "The Bishop told me himself" (I pray in what Tongue? for he speaks no English, and you no Greek, any more than your *Interpreter*, so called) "that Mr. W. desired Mr. J. to know of him if he would consecrate him Bishop?' Mr. J. solemnly declares that he never told the Bishop any such Thing. But, be that as it may, the point does not turn on the validity of ordination by a *Greek Bishop*, but on the Validity of Ordination procured by *Money* and performed in an *unknown Tongue*.

My Advice to you is, either be silent, or procure a better Defender of your Cause.

John Wesley

12 William Briggs, Letter to Charles Wesley

March 10, 1765

Source: holograph; MARC, DDPr 1/13. Image provided by The John Rylands Research Institute and Library, The University of Manchester. Material from the Methodist collection deposited at The John Rylands Research Institute and Library is used with the permission of The John Rylands University Librarian and Director of the University of Manchester Library and The Trustees for Methodist Church Purposes (The Methodist Church in Britain).

[excerpt]

There is one thing I (secretly) want to search to the bottom, but I am afraid to stir a step in it. And I will mention it to you, though I protest I want no solution from you if you should think it as well for me to be in the dark. It has been strongly rumoured here that "your brother (by Mr. [John] Jones) solicited the itinerant bishop that he would ordain him (your brother) a bishop." This your brother has, in some sort, contradicted in the public papers. Yet a very worthy man, and one of a truly upright mind, assured me that he, in conversation with Mr. Jones, asked whether Mr. Wesley approved of his (Mr. Jones's) ordination by the Greek bishop; to which Mr. Jones replied, rubbing his hands, "O to be sure; for he would gladly have been ordained a bishop by him, could it have been done." Now though it might not be altogether true as reported, yet here certainly appears to be a solid foundation to surmise that the bishop was interrogated whether he would or could ordain your brother. Now I should be extremely glad to know if your brother directly or indirectly never gave the least occasion for such an application. If anyone officiously did it of himself, or innocently enquired of the bishop how far his powers extended (without the smallest degree of authority from your brother), your dear brother has answered the charge with propriety. But if he by word, or deed, or writing gave rise to such application – this I shall be glad to be ignorant of, as the inference must be grievous to me who love[s] and honour[s] him so highly.

that our Ministers mean to act with consistence. There is one
thing I (secretly) want to search to the bottom; but I am afraid to
stir a step in it — & I will mention it to You, tho' I profess I want
no solution from You, if You should think it as well for me
to be in the dark. It has been strongly rumour'd here, that "Your
"Br. (by Mr. Jones) solicited the Itinerant Bp. that he would ordain
"him (Yr. Br.) a Bishop." This Yr. Br. has, in some sort, contradicted
in the publick papers; yet, a very worthy Man & one of a truly
upright Mind assured me, that he, in conversation with Mr.
Jones, ask'd, whether Mr. W. approv'd of his (Mr. Jones's) Ordination
by the Greek Bpd. To which Mr Jones reply'd, rubbing his hands,
"O to be sure; for he would gladly have been ordain'd a Bishop by
"him, could it have been done". Now tho' it might not be
altogether true as reported, yet here certainly appears to
be a solid foundation to surmise, that the Bp was interrogated
whether he would or could ordain Your Brother. Now I should
be extremely glad to know, if Your Bro. directly or Indirectly
never gave the least Occasion for such an application. If any
one officiously did it of himself or innocently enquired of the
Bp. how far his powers extended (without the smallest degree
of authority from Your Brother) your dear Bro. has answer'd
the charge with propriety; but if he by word or deed or writing
gave rise to such application — this I shall be glad to be igno:
:rant of, as the inference must be grievous to one who Love
& honour him so highly.

William Briggs, Letter to Charles Wesley, March 10, 1765

13 Inscription of the Play *Diotrephes and Stentor*

1765

Source: [Anonymous], *Diotrephes and Stentor: A New Farce, Acted near Moorfields* (London: 1765), p. [3].

To
ERASMUS AULONITA,
Stiling Himself
Bishop, in ARCADIA.

My Lord,

Not even *Theodore king of Corsica*[1] could be poorer than your *lordship*, when you first made your appearance, amongst certain people, as a *bishop of the Greek church*. Happy had it been for that unfortunate *monarch*, had he been possessed of your *lordship*'s sagacity; he had perhaps now been alive, instead of dying of a broken heart, under circumstances of the deepest poverty and distress. The steps your lordship took to relieve your wants, were worthy *yourself*; and we doubt not but your appearance and transactions, while in *England*, will be remembered till *knavery* itself shall be abolished, and credulity sleep secure from its devouring maw.

Had your *lordship* concealed your abilities as an author*, and had your *modesty* so far prevailed as to have concealed your *dignity as a bishop*, your *lordship's* breeches had, by this time, been hanging at the pawn-broker's, and we should probably have seen your *tail*; a discovery, at this juncture, of no small importance, as it might have saved the *French* King 6000 livres,[2] as well as prevented much mischief: for by the most certain conjecture that can be made, whenever the *wild beast*†, that since your lordship's departure across the seas

1 Theodore of Corsica (1694-1756) was a German who convinced Corsican exiles to invade their native island and crown him king. Although he acted as King of Corsica for a while, the populace eventually turned against him and forced him into exile. He died in England in 1756, the ward of Horace Walpole.

2 Perhaps a reference to Leonhard Euler (1707-1783), a Swiss mathematician and scientist who was rewarded with 6,000 livres by the King of France for one of his books. Despite his scientific contributions, Euler was pilloried as being philosophically unsophisticated by Voltaire.

has *ravaged the Gevaudan*, shall be apprehended, it will be found to be no other that your *lordship* on *all fours*.[1]

I am, Your Lordship's Most devoted

Misostasis.

* This Erasmus published a book, which he pretended to be the author of, but was not;[2] however, by means of this book, he gained the reputation of a learned writer, as well as money, from those who were induced to respect and relieve him upon that account. This a certain gentleman detected, and assured me of.

† It is imagined this wild beast is an allegorical representation of the *Jesuits*.

1 A letter of Horace Walpole dated March 26, 1765, related the story of a ferocious beast that in the previous year had killed supposedly more than a hundred people in the region of Gévaudan in southern France: *The Letters of Horace Walpole, the Earl of Orford* (6 vols.; London: Richard Bentley, 1840), 5:13 and the note accompanying it on that page.

2 In reference to the English (Haberkorn) printing of *Petra tou Skandalou* (see above). Gerasimos signed the work as the author of the introduction. However, the fact that the name of the author (Meniatis) was omitted from the publication could give readers the impression that Gerasimos claimed authorship for it.

14 Letter of Gerasimos Avlonites to Petrus Nicolaus Filenius, Bishop of Linköping[3]

Between 1761 and 1780, August 13, 1768 [or 1764]

Source: Manuscript letter in the Linköping Public Library (Bibliotekarie Linköpings kommun) identified as "Petrus Filenius (E005/Br 22)".

TRANSCRIPTION

Viro
Reverendissimo, ac Domino Fratri in
Christo
Episcopo Linkjopensis
Longe Honoratissimo
Doctori S.S. Theologiae celeberimo

Has meas litteras spero, ut sereno vultu perlegas et benigna manu accipias humillime peto. Ipsae hae litterae nil aliud sunt, quam sanctum erga Te observantiae et pietatis testimonium Deum testor Vir Reverendissime. Rogo, pro humanitate et benignitate tua christiana si velis excusa aliquid, ἵνα ποίησις ἔλεος ut iter meum in Stoholmia juvante Deo continuare possim, atque idem hoc est quod iterum iterumque abs te peto quam humillime πίστευσον ὅτι μῆ ἔχω μόνον ἐν Χριστόν ἅπερ δεδοκέμος ἡ φιλανθρωποίαν τῆς ἡμετέρας. Deus noster duplicem hanc gratiam benedictione sua diurna centies et millies remunerabitur, et audiet preces meas ex vera fide in Christum perfecte,[4]

3 Petrus Nicolaus Filenius (1704-1780) received a doctorate in theology from Lund University in 1730 and in the next year became a lecturer in the Royal Academy of Turku and in 1735 was made professor of oriental languages there and in 1741 professor of theology. In 1742 he became professor of oriental and Greek languages in Lund and became a Member of the Swedish Parliament in 1746. He was appointed Bishop of Linköping and served in that role through 1771.

4 The word *perfecte* appears at the bottom of the first page and then repeated at the top of the second page.

certo a Deo exaudiuntur et implentur pro Te Totaque Familia Tua Praenobilissima, propter Christum cujus bonitati Te, me vero et petitiones meas piisime comendo et permaneo,

Nominis Tui Reverendissimi

εἰς ἀθανάτου εὐλαβιάς
Τεκμήριον
Καὶ ἀδελφὸν ἐν Χριστῶ
Erasmus Aulonita Episcopus
Arcadiae in Candia

Linkjoping die XIII Agusti
1768 [or 1764][1]

TRANSLATION

Most Reverend Sir,
Distinguished Brother in Christ,
Bishop of Linköping,
Most Honored
and Celebrated Doctor of Sacred Theology

I most humbly ask that you receive this letter with a serene countenance and with a kind hand. This letter is nothing more than a witness, God being the witness, most reverend sir, of your reverence and your piety. I ask, for the sake of your humanity and your Christian kindness, if you can excuse something [Greek] that you may do mercy, [Latin] that, God helping, I may be able to continue my journey to Stockholm, and the same, that is, again and again I ask you most humbly [Greek] as a faithful one, for I have nothing at all but Christ himself, given only philanthropy between us. [Latin] May our God by his divine blessing repay you double for this blessing, a hundredfold, a thousandfold, and may he hear my prayers (for whenever our prayers [come] completely from true faith in Christ,

1 I read the Arabic numeral as "8" with the top loop open, though it's also possible that it could be "4". Gerasimos was in Britain and Holland much of the year 1764 so it seems more likely to be "8".

Viro
Reverendissimo, ac Domino Fratri in
Christo
Episcopo Linkjopensis
Longe Honoratissimo
Doctori S.S. Theologiæ celeberimo.

Has meas, Litteras spero, ut sereno Vultu per:
legas et benigna manu accipias humillime
peto. Ipsæ hæ litteræ nil aliud sunt, quam
Sanctum erga Te observantiæ et pietatis testimo:
nium Deum testor Vir Reverendissime. rogo,
pro humanitate et benignitate Tua Christiana
si velis ex casa aliquid, ἵνα ποίησας ἔχε ut
iter meum in Stokolmia juvante Deo conti:
nuare possim, atque idem hoc est, quod iterum
iterumque abs Te peto quam humillime.
πίστευσον ὅτι οὐκ ἔχω μόνον ἓν χρυσίον ἄπερ
δεδομένος ἡ φιλανθρωπίαν τῆς ἡμετέρας.
Deus noster duplicem hanc gratiam benedic:
tione sua divina centies et millies remune:
rabitur, et audiet preces meas, quia quando
nostræ preces ex vera fide in Christum per
fectæ,

Letter of Gerasimos Avlonites to Petrus Nicolaus Filenius, Bishop of Linköping, between 1761 and 1780, August 13, 1768 [or 1764]

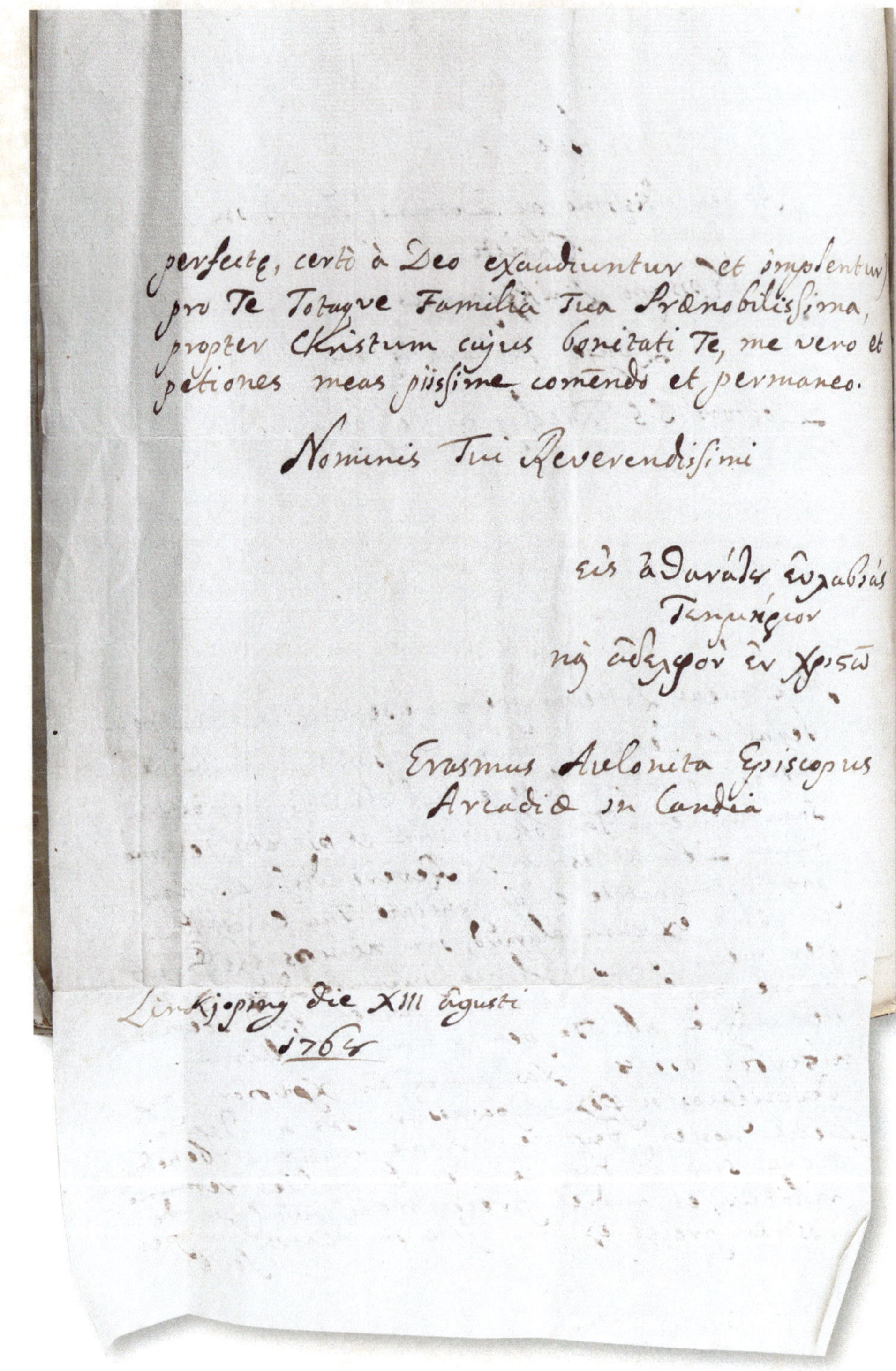

perfecte, certo à Deo exaudiuntur et implentur)
pro Te Totaque Familia tua Praenobilissima,
propter Christum cujus bonitati Te, me vero et
petiones meas piissime comendo et permaneo.

Nominis Tui Reverendissimi

εἰς ἀθανάτην εὐλαβείας
Ταπεινότερον
καὶ ἀδελφὸν ἐν Χριστῷ

Erasmus Avlonita Episcopus
Arcadiæ in Candia

Linkjöping die XIII Augusti
1768

Letter of Gerasimos Avlonites to Petrus Nicolaus Filenius, Bishop of Linköping, between 1761 and 1780, August 13, 1768 [or 1764]

it is certain they are heard and fulfilled by God) for You and for Your Most Noble Family, through Christ by whose goodness I most piously commend You and my own petitions, and I remain

Of your Most Reverend Name,

to the praises of the Immortal,
a witness
and a brother in Christ
Erasmus Aulonita Bishop
Of Arcadia in Candia [Herakleion]

Linköping, the 13th day of August
1764 [or 1768]

15 Letter of Gerasimos Avlonites to the President of the Church Council of Stockholm

March 29, 1769.

Source: Transcription by Börje Knös, in "Επισκεψη Κρητικου Έπισκοπου στη Σουηδια τον ιζ' Άϊωνα" ("Visit of a Cretan Bishop to Sweden in the Eighteenth Century") in Κρητικά Χρονικά 3:1 (1961-2) 61-62. Knös's transcription is released with the permission of the Society of Cretan Historical Studies, which publishes Κρητικά Χρονικά. The text given in Κρητικά Χρονικά does not give images of this letter. The current location of this manuscript is unknown; Knös reported that it was in the archives of the Church Council of Stockholm.

TRANSCRIPTION

Reverendissime Doctissime Domine
SS Theologiae Doctor Celeberrime
Τὰ πρὸς ζωὴν καὶ εὐσέβειαν ἀπὸ Χριστοῦ
δεόμενος

Erasmus Aulonita Episcopus Ecclesiae Graecae.

Ego, Deo volente, die solis ex Holmiae abire et per Justadium in Germaniam navigare mecum constitui, sed hoc est officium, ἵνα εὐχαριστήσω τοὺς ἐυεργέτας, προτοῦ πορευόμενος. Hoc est summo studio, ut recordamur benevolentia illius quae erga nos fecerunt. Ἡ εὐχαριστία ἔστι ἄξια πράγματι, ὅταν μὲ καθαρὰν καρδίαν ἐργάζεται ὁ ἄνθρωπος, ὑποδεικνύουσα αὐτω τὴν ὁδὸυ τῆς ταπεινώσεως, ἀλλὰ ἡ ἀχαριστία φέρουσα ὕβριν. Oportet enim eum, qui exoptat amicus Dei esse, conservare hoc, τοῦτο ἔστι, ἵνα γινώσκεις πάνδοτες τὸν εὐεργέτην τοῦ. Λοιπόν, precor autem dominum Jesum, verum Deum et hominem, toto pectore, ut in vos universos et singulos, Doctores Ecclesiae Dei, vestrosque liberos et familias affatim e coelo omne genus benedictionum suarum effundat. Faxit Deus, ut in pace et tranquillitate utrumque regimen ad gloriam divinae majestatis et Ecclesiae salutem diu administrare queatis. ἐῤῥωσο ἐν Χριστῷ.

P. S. Hoc volo ab te petere, Vir reverendissime, pro humanitate et benignitate tua Christiana, si velis mihi scribere litteras commendaticias in itinere meo ad pastoribus Ecclesiae Dei, ut fiat promptitudo animi et sollicit(udo) ad procurandum equos et currus, non gratis, sed eum pecunia mea, quia lingua suecana non est mihi nota, et rustici non intelligunt mihi, et possum manere per multos dies in itinere. Credo et spero hoc non est difficultas nullum, te vir reverendissime.

Holmiae die 29 Martii 1769.

Cultor humillissimus
ὁ ἀδελφὸς ἐν Χριστῷ

TRANSLATION

Most Reverend and Most Learned Sir,
Celebrated Doctor of Sacred Theology,
having been given all that is needed for life and godliness from Christ[1]

Erasmus Aulonita, a Bishop of the Greek Church.

[Latin] I have decided, God willing, to leave Stockholm on Sunday to sail to Germany by way of Ystad, and my duty now is to thank my benefactors before I go. This is of the utmost importance as we recall the benevolence of those who have done good on our behalf. [Greek] Thanksgiving is an appropriate act when one acts with a clean heart, showing him the way of humility, but failure to give thanks bears hubris. [Latin] It is appropriate, then, for one who wants to be a friend of God to hold on to this: [Greek] to show hospitality to your benefactor. So [Latin] I pray the Lord Jesus Christ, truly God and truly human, with my whole heart, that to each and every one of you who are teachers of the Church of God and your children and your families, God may pour out all manner of his blessings. May God grant that in peace and tranquility you will be able to administer both areas of governance: for the glory of the divine majesty, and the salvation of the church. Be strong in Christ! P.S. This I wish to ask of you, most reverend sir, for your Christian humanity and kindness, if you might write a commendatory letter for me in my journey to the

1 II Peter 1:3, cited in Greek.

pastors of the Church of God, that there may be readiness of mind and care for procuring horses and carriages, not for free, but with my own money, because I do not know the Swedish language and the local folks do not understand me, and I might take many days on the journey. I believe and hope this is not any difficulty for you, reverend sir.

Stockholm, the 29th day of March, 1769

your most humble follower,
[and] brother in Christ

16 Letter of Gerasimos Avlonites to Bishop Johan Engeström, Bishop of Lund, Sweden

July 17, 1769

Source: Transcription by Börje Knös in "Επισκεψη Κρητικου Επισκοπου στη Σουηδια τον ιζ' Αἰωνα" ("Visit of a Cretan Bishop to Sweden in the Eighteenth Century") in Κρητικα Χρονικα 3:1 (1961-2) 63-64, checked against accompanying negative mages of the manuscript. Knös's transcription is released with the permission of the Society of Cretan Historical Studies, which publishes Κρητικα Χρονικα. The current whereabouts of this manuscript is unknown.

TRANSCRIPTION

Τῷ πιστῷ τοῦ Κυρίου ἡμῶν Ἰησοῦ Χριστοῦ
ἀιδεσιμωτάτῳ τε καὶ ἐυσεβεστάτῳ
Κυρίῳ Κυρίῳ
Διδασκάλῳ
Τῆς ἁγίας θεολογίας καὶ ἐπισκόπῳ
ἀξιωτάτῳ
Τὰ πρὸς ζωὴν καὶ ἐυσέβειαν ἀπὸ Χριστοῦ δεόμενος.

ἀπὸ ἐνθάδε τῆ ιζ Ιούλlου
αψξθ.

Ὁ πολέμος κατ' οὐδενὸς παύεται πολεμῶν, ὁ σατανὰς δὲ ἄσπλαγχνος ἐστί καὶ μισάνθρωπος· διὸ καὶ παντὶ ἀνθρώπω πολεμεῖν ὀυκ ὀκνεῖ . Λοιπῶν ὀφείλομεν ζητῆναι καὶ εὕρομεν τὴν παράκλησιν τοῦ πνεύματος, μὴ δάκρυα καὶ πένθος καὶ στεναγμὸν. Ταᾶτα, εἀν μὴ τις ἄνθρωπος ἔχει πρὸ ὀφθαλμῶν τηὴν χαρὰν καὶ τὴν ἐλπίδα, ὅτι μέλλει λυτρώσεως τυγχάνειν καὶ ζωῆς, ὅν δύναται ὑπομένειν τὰς θλίψεις, οὔτε τὸ φορτίον καὶ τὴν στενὴν ὁδὸν ἀναδέξασθαι. Ἡ γὰρ συνοῦσα ἐλπὶς καὶ χαρὰ ποιεῖ ἀυτὸν κάμνειν καὶ ὑπομένειν τὰς θλίψεις καὶ τὸ φορτίον καὶ τὴν στενὴν ὁδὸν ἀναδέξασται. Καὶ γὰρ ἐπὶ τοῦ Ἰώβ, ἐι ᾖδει, ὅτι εἰς τοῦς πειρασμοὺς ἐμπεςὼν μέλλει ὑπομένειν. οὐ γὰρ ἀγνοοῦσα, ὅτι εἰς τὰς θλίψεις οἱ σπείρουτες ἐν δάκρυσιν, ἐν ἀγαλλιάσει θεριοῦσιν. Ἐνθυμοῦμενος ὅτι αὐτὸς ὁ Χριστὸς τὸν αἰῶνα τοῦτον οὕτω διώδευσεν, ὀνειδιζόμενος, διωκόμενος, ἐμπαιζόμενος, τέλος καὶ ἀτίμω θανάτω διὰ σταυροῦ τελειούμενος.[1]

1 Ps. 125:5 LXX (126:5 in English versions).

ἰδον ὁ θεὸς τὴν τυραννίδα καὶ μοχθηρὰν ζωῆν τοῦ πασᾶ ἐν νήσω καὶ μᾶλλον τὰ δάκρυα ἐκ πολλῆς θλίψεως καὶ συνοχῆς καρδία(ς) τοῦ χρυσονίμου λαοῦ; Διὰ προστάγματος τοῦ βασιλέως, ἀποστελόμενω(ν) αὐτῶν ἐν αἰγύπτω ὥσπερ τύραννων, ἐλπίζοντας ὁ ἀσεβεὰς ἵνα νικήσοι τοὺς αἰγυπτίους, ἀλλὰ θεικόν ἐνεργοῦν ἐν πάση δυνάμ(ει) ἀπέκτειναν αὐτὸν ὁι Ἀιγυπτίοι. Ἀληθὸς, αὐτὴ ἡ θεία δύναμις ἀπέκτεινεν αὐτὸν. Τριάκοντα ἔτη τυραννούμενοι οἱ χριστιανοὶ ἀπὸ ἀυτοὺ. Διὰ τοῦτο καὶ ἐγῶ θλίψις καὶ πόνος καὶ ξένος ἐκ πατρίδος γενόμενος, κατά τὸν προφήτην, λέγουσαν, ὡμοιώθην πελεκανῖ ἐρημικῷ, ἐγενήθην ὡσεὶ νυκτικόραξ ἐν ὀικοπέδω, ἐγενόμην ὡς στρουθίον μονόζωον ἐπὶ δώματος.[1] Πάλιν ὁ προφήτης φησι, οὕτως ὁ πτωχὸς ἐκέκραξε καὶ ὁ Κύριος ἐισήκουσεν αὐτοῦ, καὶ ἐκ πασῶν τῶν θλίψεων ἀυτοῦ ἔσωσεν ἀυτὸν.[2]

Δόξα τῶ ἀγίῳ Θεῷ, ἐπιστολὴ ἔλαβον ἐκ νήσου Κρήτη in Holmiae εκ πόλεως Amstelodami, ἵνα ἐπανακάμψω ἐν τῆ ἐπάρχιά μου. Παραυτίκα πορευόμενος πρὸς τοὺς διδασκάλους Consistoriales, καὶ ἐπιστολὴ λαβόν συστατικὴν περὶ ζωῆς καὶ πρᾶξης καὶ διαγωγῆς ἐν ὅσω καιρῷ ἐκάθισα ἐν Holmiae.

Οὐ ἐπιλανθάνῳ τὰς χάριτας, ἐνεργεσίας, φιλοξενίας καὶ μᾶλλον φιλανθρωπίας τὴς ἐυγενεστάτης Κυρίας ἀδελφοις τῆς ὑμετέρας, τοῦτο ἐστι ἡ γυνὴ τοῦ αἰδεσιμωτάτου Praepositi Munthe ἐν Malmungiae. Ἀλγέω περ᾿ τῷ θάνατῳ τοῦ μακαρίτου ἀδελφοῦ ὑμῶν, Praepositus τῶ ὄντι μακάριος καὶ ζηλωτοὶς τοῦ βίου, ἐπειδὴ διὰ θερμῆς καὶ φιλαρέτου διαγωγῆς τὸ πολίτευμα ἐν οὐρανοῖς εἴχεν. Ἡ γὰρ ἀξία τὰ Παθήματα τοῦ νῦν καιροῦ πρός τὴν μέλλουσαν δόξαν ἀποκαλυφθῆναι εἰς ημᾶς.[3] Deus et Pater Domini nostri Jesu Christi te in provecta ista aetate et animi corporisque robore benignissime servet suae in primis gloriae et bonis, mihi vere hunc animum tuum benevolum, quem erga me geris.

Προσεύχον, ἀιδεσιμώτατε, περὶ ἐμοῦ, ἵνα ὁ θεὸς, ταῖς θλίψεσι καὶ τοῖς παθήμασι ἀγαλλιάσοι ἡ ψυχῆ μου. Sicut et Paulus epistolas suas precationibus terminavit, et quando nostrae preces ex vera fide Christum proiectae, certo a Deo exaudiuntur et implentur. ἐρρώσο.

Nominis Tui Reverendissimi
cultor humillissimus
Erasmus Aulonita Episcopus
Ecclesiae Graecae

1 Ps. 101:7-8 LXX (102:6-7 in English versions).

2 Ps. 33:6 LXX (34:6 in English versions).

3 Roman. 8:18.

TRANSLATION

To the Faithful of Our Lord Jesus Christ
Most Venerable and Reverent
Honorable Teacher of Sacred Theology
and Most Worthy Bishop
having been given all that is needed for life and godliness from Christ[4]

From here [Stockholm?], the 17th of July, 1769

The fighter never ceases from fighting, for Satan is merciless and a hater of humankind, so he does not hesitate to fight with everyone. So then we ought to seek and find the comfort of the Spirit, not weeping or mourning or crying. Unless one has before one's eyes the joy and the hope that the reality of redemption and life is coming, one cannot endure the tribulations, nor bear the burden and the narrow road. For present hope and joy makes one able to be weary and to endure the tribulations and bear the burden and the narrow way. So it was with Job, as you know, who, falling into temptations, is able to persevere. For is it not known that what is sown in tears is reaped in joy?[5] Consider that Jesus Christ, having repulsed, reproached, pursued, and mocked this present age, through the cross accomplished a goal that was not worthy of death.

God seeing the tyranny and the hard life on the island, the tears of tribulation and the heartfelt grief of his precious people, by an order of the king, as soon as the tyrants had been sent into Egypt, hoping that [their] impiety might defeat the Egyptians, but [θεικον?] acting with all strength, the Egyptians killed him. Christians were tyrannized by him for thirty years. Truly the divine power itself killed him. For this reason I too suffered tribulations and pain and became an exile from my country, according to the prophet, saying, "I am like a pelican in the desert, like an owl of the desert, like a lone sparrow on the rooftop."[6]

4 II Peter 1:3.
5 Ps. 125:5 LXX (126:5 in English versions).
6 Ps. 101:7-8 LXX (102:6-7 in English versions).

Again the prophet said, "Thus the poor man cried out, and the Lord saved him out of all his tribulations."[1]

Thanks to holy God I have in Stockholm a letter from the Island of Crete [forwarded] from the city of Amsterdam, that I should return to my province [eparchy]. I am coming immediately to the consistorial teachers (instructors) with a commendatory letter concerning my life and actions and conduct in the time I have spent in Stockholm.

I am not forgetting the gifts, the good deeds, the acts of hospitality, and especially the kindness of the most noble lady, our sister, that is, the wife of the most esteemed Dean [*praepositus*] Munthe of Malmö. I grieve over the death of the blessed brother the Dean who was indeed blessed and zealous of life; because his warmth and virtuous life, he now has citizenship in heaven. For, "the sufferings of the present age are not worthy of the coming glory to be revealed in us" (Romans 8:18). May the God and Father of our Lord Jesus Christ preserve you in this coming age, in body and spirit, in the first good fruits of glory, indeed, that benevolent spirit that you showed to me.

I prayed, excellent one, concerning myself, that God [would change] the sufferings of my soul into joy. [Latin] Thus Paul ended his letters with prayers, and when our prayers put forth Christ from true faith, it is certain they will be heard and fulfilled by God. Be strong!

the most humble follower
of your reverend name,
Erasmus Aulonita, Bishop
of the Greek Church

1 Ps. 33:6 LXX (34:6 in English versions).

17 Letter of Gerasimos Avlonites to Johann Kaspar Lavater

December 16, 1772

Source: This and the following five letters are held in the Central Library of Zurich (Zentralbibliothek Zurich). This manuscript is identified as 'FA Lav. Ms. 501.146'.

TRANSCRIPTION

Viro
Honoratissimo Domino, Diacono
Καὶ ἀδελφῶ ἐν Χριστῷ

Has meas litteras, spero ut sereno vultu perlegas ac benigna manu accipias humillime peto. Ipsae hae litterae nil aliud sunt, quam ut tibi notum faciam ὅτι ἀδύνατω ἐστι ἵνα ἐλθῶ πρὸς τὴν ἡμετέραν ἡμῶν ἀγάπην. Τὰ ἱμάτια καὶ ὁ πώγων, mihi impediunt. si velis pro humanitate et benignitate tua christiana ad me venires, gratia mihi erit, et si non velis παρακαλῶ δηλοςῶν μοι τοῦτο, ἵνα δύναμαι πορευθίνε, ἐρρώσο.

εἰς ἀθανάτου εὐλαβίας
Ἐράσιμος πρωπρ. Ἀρκαδης
ἐπίσκοπος ὁ κερκυρίος

τῆ xvi δεκεμβριου
αψοβ.
1772

146

2

Viro
Honoratissimo, Domino, Diacono
καὶ ἀδελφῷ ἐν Χριστῷ

Has meas Litteras, spero ut sereno Vultu perlegas et benigna manu accipias humillime peto. Ipsæ hæ Litteræ nil aliud
sunt, quam ut Tibi notum faciam, ὅτι ἀδύνατον ἐστι
ἵνα ἔλθω πρὸς τὴν ὑμετέραν ἡμῶν ἀγάπην. Τὰ [illegible]
καὶ ὁ χειμών, mihi impediunt. si velis pro humanitate et
benignitate Tua Christiana ad me venires; gratu mihi
erit. et si non velis παρακαλῶ δηλοποιήσεις τοῦτο, ἵνα
δύναμαι πορευθῆναι, ἔρρωσο.

εἰς ἀθανάτου εὐλαβείας
Γεράσιμος [illegible]
ἐπίσκοπος ὁ [illegible]

15.
τῇ XVI Δεκεμβρίου
αψοβ.
1772

271

Letter of Gerasimos Avlonites to Johann Kaspar Lavater, December 16, 1772

TRANSLATION

To the Most Honorable Sir, Deacon
and Brother in Christ,

I hope you can read this letter with a serene countenance and I most humbly ask that you receive it with a kind hand. This letter is nothing more than to let you know that I am not able to come to your dinner. [My] clothes and [my] beard embarrass me. If you would by your kindness and Christian humanity come to me, it will be a gift to me, and if you do not wish this, please clarify this for me, that I may proceed. Be strong!

Unto the Praises of the Immortal,
Erasimos Protopresbyter Bishop of Arcadia
from Corfu

The 16th of December
1772

18 Letter of Gerasimos Avlonites to Johann Kaspar Lavater

December 18, 1772

Source: Central Library of Zurich manuscript 'FA Lav. Ms. 501.145'.

TRANSCRIPTION

Τῷ πιστῷ καὶ ἀγαπητῷ ἐν Χριστῷ
Τιμοτάτῳ καὶ Χρυσημωτάτῳ Διακόνῳ
Κυρίῳ Κυρίῳ Lavert καὶ ἀδελφῶ
ἔν Χριστῷ
τὰ πρὸς ζωὴν καὶ εὐσέβειαν ἀπὸ Χριστοῦ δεόμενος

Λύπημος ἐστὶ μεγάλη, καὶ ἀδιαλείπτος ὀδύνη τῆ καρδία μου, περὶ τὴς ἀσθένηας τῆς χρυσημωτάτοις Κυρίας γυνή σου. ἀλήθειαν λέγω ἐν Χριστῷ καὶ οὐ ψεύδομαι. Τοῦτο καὶ ἡ αδέλφος μου λυπούμενος; ἀλλὰ ἐυχόμενος τὸν θεὸν περὶ τῆς ιἄσεος αὐτοὶς. δόξασον, ἀγαπητὲ τὸν θεὸν, ἐυχαρίστισον τὸν δεσπότην, διό τι, χωρὶς ἐμοῦ, οὐ δύνασθε ποιεῖν οὐδὲν, λέγει ὁ Χριστὸς. ἀγαπῶ ἐπιθυμῶ ἵνα ἀκούσω σήμερον πῶς ἐυρισκόμενος. Κύριος διφυλάξαι αὐτοὶν, Κύριος βοηθήσαι ἀυτοὶν, ἐπὶ κλίνης ὀδύνης, καὶ ἐπιστρέψοι ἡ ἀρρωσία ἀυτοὶς, καὶ ιἄσοι αὐτοὶν. ἡ ἀδελφός μου ἀσπάζεται τὴν κυρίαν ἐν φιλήματι ἁγίω. Πᾶσαν τὴν μέριμναν, ἀγαπητὲ, ἀπορριψον εἰς Ιησοῦν Χριστὸν, καὶ αὐτὸς μέλει περὶ ἡμῶν. ἀγάπα με ἐν τῷ τόπῳ τῶν ἐκλεκτῶν. ἐρρώσο.

εἰς ἀθανάτου εὐλαβίας
Ἐράσιμος πρωπρ. Ἀρκαδης ἐπισκοπος
ὁ κερκυρίος

Τῆ ,ιη Δεκος
α.ψ.ο.β.

Letter of Gerasimos Avlonites to Johann Kaspar Lavater, December 18, 1772

TRANSLATION

To the Faithful and Beloved in Christ
Most Esteemed and Most Excellent Deacon
The Honorable Lavert [*sic*], a Brother in Christ
having been given all that is needed for life and godliness from Christ[1]

There is great sadness and unceasing pain in my heart concerning the illness of your excellent lady and wife. I speak the truth in Christ and I am not lying: this is also the pain of my brother, but I beg God for her healing. Praise, love God, thank the Master, because, "Without me, you can do nothing," says Christ. I would love and desire to hear how she has been found today. May the Lord keep her, may the Lord help her on her bed of pain, and may her illness turn away and she be healed. May my brother greet the lady with a holy kiss. Beloved, let every worry be driven to Jesus Christ[2] and he will come for you. Love me among those who are elect. Be strong!

Unto the Praises of the Immortal,
Erasimos Protopr[esbyter] Bishop of Arkadia
from Corfu

The 18th of December
1772

1 II Peter 1:3.
2 I Peter 5:7.

19 Letter of Gerasimos Avlonites to Johann Kaspar Lavater

December 26, 1772

Source: Central Library of Zurich manuscript 'FA Lav. Ms. 501.147'.

TRANSCRIPTION

Τῷ πιστῷ καὶ ἀγαπητῷ
ἀδελφῷ ἐν Χριστῷ
Χαίρον.
Τὰ πρὸς ζωὴν καὶ εὐσέβειαν ἀπὸ Χριστοῦ
δεόμενος
Ἐράσιμος πρωπρ. Ἀρκαδης ἐπισκοπος
Αὐλονήτις

Ἐπιποθεῖ ἡ ψυχή μου ἀγαπητὲ, ἵνα ἀκούσω περὶ τὴς ὑγείας τὴς εὐγενεστατης Κυίιας γυνή σου. Κα᾽ μᾶλλον ἡ ἀδελφή μου τοῦτο ἐπιποθεῖ. οὐκ ἐπιλωνθάνομαι ἕος θανάτου τὰς χάριτας καὶ εὐεργέσιας ὕπερ [ἅπερ?] ἔλαβον ἀπὸ σου Κύριε καὶ ἀδελφὲ ἐν Χριστῶ. In Christi manu et potestate esse nostram vitam et salutem aeternam: ipse enim chirographum quod nobis adversum erat cui affixit et disrupit: ipse est caelestis Patris cancellarius, qui chirographum nos ad mortem obligatus ita induxit ut nullum vestigium maneat eius quod delectum est. Quare quisquis vult chirographum suum, quo ad satisfactionem pro peccatis obligatus est, deleri et irritum reddi, is ad solum Christum confugiat: et quoniam omnis spes et fiducia vita in Christo est, quoniam per ipsum peccatum deletum et mors devicta Christum solum sequatur si in Christo est ambulandum fidelibus tum ipse solus est via qua per veritatem ad vitam pervenitur sempiternam. ἀσπὰζου τὴν ἐυγενεστᾶτην κυρίαν γυνῆ σου ἐν φιλήματοι ἁγίω. ἀσπάζου πάντας τοὺς φίλους καὶ ἀδελφοὺς ἐν Χριστω. ἀσπάζου τὴν ἐκκλησίαν τοῦ Χριστοῦ ἀυξάνοντες ἐν χάριτι καὶ γνῶσει τοῦ κυρίου ἡμῶν καὶ σωτῆρος Ιησοῦ Χριστοῦ.

P. S. θαυμάζω ἀγαπητὲ ὅτι οὐκ ἐλᾶβα τὴν παλεὰ διαθήκην, λιπὸν ἀγαπητὲ εἀν μὲ ἀγάπας; περὶψὼ μοι ἀυτὴν καθὸς ὑποσχάσθις. σὺ ἀγαπητὲ, μὲ ἔδοκες ἀπὸ κάρδιας τὴν παλεὰν διαθήκη, ἐλπίζω ὅτι καὶ ἀπὸ καρδίας ἵνα πέμψοις αὐτὴν εἰς χεῖρα τοῦ κυρίου Bernner, ἀδελφοῦ ἐν Χριστῶ, ταῦτα ἐρρώσο. γράψων ἵνα ακούσω περὶ τὴς ὑγείας τὴς κυρίας.

Basilea die xxvi Dris
1772

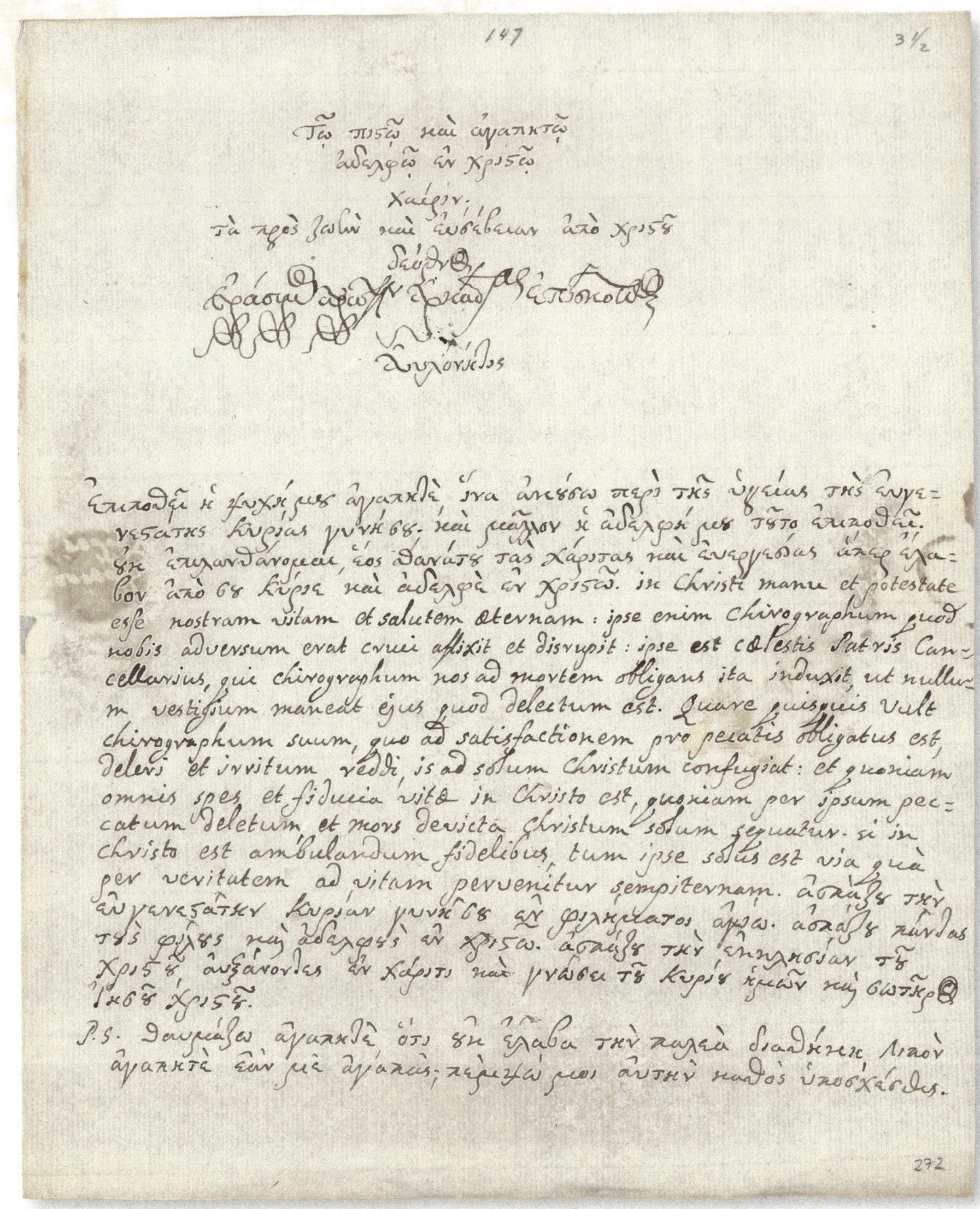

147 3½

Τῷ πιστῷ καὶ ἀγαπητῷ
ἀδελφῷ ἐν Χριστῷ
χαίρειν.
τὰ πρὸς ζωὴν καὶ εὐσέβειαν ἀπὸ Χριστοῦ
δεόμενος
Γεράσιμος [illegible] ἐπίσκοπος [illegible]
Αὐλωνίτης

Ἐπιποθεῖ ἡ ψυχή μου ἀγαπητέ, ἵνα ἀκούσω περὶ τῆς ὑγείας τῆς εὐγε=
νεστάτης κυρίας γυναικός σου· καὶ μᾶλλον ἡ ἀδελφή μου τοῦτο ἐπιποθεῖ.
οὐκ ἐπιλανθάνομαι, ἕως θανάτου τὰς χάριτας καὶ εὐεργεσίας ἅπερ ἔλα=
βον ἀπὸ σοῦ κύριε καὶ ἀδελφὲ ἐν Χριστῷ. in Christi manu et potestate
esse nostram vitam et salutem æternam: ipse enim chirographum quod
nobis adversum erat cruci affixit et disrupit: ipse est cœlestis Patris Can=
cellarius, qui chirographum nos ad mortem obligans ita induxit, ut nullu=
m vestigium maneat ejus quod delectum est. Quare quisquis vult
chirographum suum, quo ad satisfactionem pro peccatis obligatus est,
deleri et irritum reddi, is ad solum Christum confugiat: et quoniam
omnis spes et fiducia vitæ in Christo est, quoniam per ipsum pec=
catum deletum et mors devicta Christum solum sequatur. si in
Christo est ambulandum fidelibus, tum ipse solus est via qua
per veritatem ad vitam pervenitur sempiternam. ἄσπασαι τὴν
εὐγενεστάτην κυρίαν γυναῖκά σου ἐν φιλήματι ἁγίῳ. ἄσπασαι πάντας
τοὺς φίλους καὶ ἀδελφοὺς ἐν Χριστῷ. ἄσπασαι τὴν ἐκκλησίαν τοῦ
Χριστοῦ, αὐξάνοντες ἐν χάριτι καὶ γνώσει τοῦ κυρίου ἡμῶν καὶ σωτῆρος
Ἰησοῦ Χριστοῦ.

P.S. θαυμάζω ἀγαπητέ, ὅτι οὐκ ἔλαβα τὴν παλαιὰν διαθήκην λαόν
ἀγαπητέ ἐὰν με ἀγαπᾷς, πέμψω μοι αὐτὴν καθὼς ὑπεσχέθης.

272

Letter of Gerasimos Avlonites to Johann Kaspar Lavater, December 26, 1772

TRANSLATION

To the Faithful and Beloved
Brother in Christ,
Greeting!
having all that is needed for life and godliness from Christ[1]
Erasimos Protopresbyter Bishop of Arcadia
Avlonites

My soul longs to hear, beloved, about the health of the noble lady, your wife, and longs that my sister is better. I shall not forget as long as I live the charity and hospitality that I have received from you, sir, [my] brother in Christ. [Latin] In Christ's hand and power is our life and eternal salvation, for he is himself the signature given for us against that which weakens and shatters us. He is himself the gatekeeper of the heavenly Father who gave us, bound as he was to death, his signature, so that no vestige might remain of that which has been destroyed. For this reason, whoever wishes his signature, by which he was bound to be a satisfaction for [our] sins that are to be destroyed and rendered void, must flee to Christ alone. And because all [our] hope and trust is life in Christ, because sin has been destroyed and death defeated, Christ alone must be followed if in Christ we walk with the faithful, then he alone is the way by which one comes through the truth to eternal life. [Greek] Greet the noble Lady your wife with a holy kiss. Greet all the friends and brothers in Christ. Greet the church of Christ, those that are increasing in the love and knowledge of our Lord and Savior Jesus Christ.

P. S. I am puzzled, beloved, that I have not received the Old Testament, so beloved do you love me? Send it to me as you promised. You, beloved, promised[2] the Old Testament with your whole heart, so I hope you will send it by the hand of Mr. Brenner [Bernner?], our brother in Christ, so be strong! Write that I may hear about the health of your lady.

Basel, the 26th day of December
1772

1 II Peter 1:3.

2 Apparently using the verb δοκειν with the sense "to promise"; see also the first Greek sentence of the next letter.

20 Letter of Gerasimos Avlonites to Johann Kaspar Lavater

December 28, 1772

Source: Central Library of Zurich manuscript 'FA Lav. Ms. 501.148'.

TRANSCRIPTION

Viro
Reverendo Domino Diacono
Καὶ ἀδελφῶ ἐν Χριστῶ
Χαίρε

Βασιλὲα τη κη Δεκεμβριου 1772

Non possum comprehendere quare non misisti Biblia Sacra in Basilea sicut tua promesione. σὺ ἀγαπητὲ δέδοκες ἐξ ὅλις τῆς καρδίας, εἰς μνημόσυγω, καὶ νῦν οὐκ [ο]ἴδα αὐτὴν. ἀκίκωα εκ στόματος τοῦ ἀδελφοῦ ἐν Χριστῶ, κυρίου Brenner, ὅτι ἡ χρυσημωτάτοι κυρία γυνή σου ἐστίν βέλτιον, καὶ περύληπος τῶν καρδίων εὑρισκόμεος. ἐλπίζω ὅτι ἡ λύπη σου ἐις χαρὰν ἐλθεὶν. σὺ γινώσκοις ἀγαπὴτε ὅτι ὁ γλυκίτατος Ιησοῦς Χριστὸς, εἶναι ἡ ὁδὸς, ἡ ζωή, καὶ ἡ ἀλήθεια καὶ ὁ Ἰατρὸς, καὶ οὐκ ἀφήσοί σε ὀρφανῶ. ἐγὼ πορευόμενος εἰς μπέρνα, καὶ ἐὰν ἀγαπὰς καὶ θέλεις ἀπὸ καρδίας ἵνα πέμψίς μου τὴν παλεὰν διαθήκη, εἴς βασιλέαν, εἰς τὸν κύριον Brenner καλὸς ἐστι, εἰδε καὶ οὐκ θέλεις εὐχαριστῶ, πάλιν σε ἀγαπῷ καὶ φιλῶ ἀπὸ καρδίας. ἀσπὰζου τὴν κυρίαν γυνή σου ἐν Φιλήματι ἀγάπης. Τοῦτο ποιὴ καὶ ἡ ἀδελφή μου. ἀσπάζου τοὺς φίλους καὶ τὴν ἐκκλίσιαν τοῦ Χριστοῦ. ὁ θεὸς τὴς ὑπομονῆς καὶ τὴς παρακλήσεως δώση σου ἵνα πάντα τὰ ἐρχόμενα τοῦ ἀνθρώπου, εἶτε καλλὰ, εἰτε ἀγαθὰ, εἰτε κακὰ, ἵνα δοξάζης τὸν θεὸν καὶ πατέρα τοῦ κυρίου ἡμῶν Ἰησοῦ Χριστοῦ. ἀρρώσο.

ὁ ἀδελφὸς ἐν Χριστῶ
Ἐράσιμος αὐλονήτις ἐπίσκοπος

ἐὰν ἀγαπὰς γράψε ἐπιστλὴ εἰς Berna,
ἵνα ἀκούσω τὰ περὶ τὴς κυρίας

Viro
Reverendo Domino Diacono
καὶ ἀδελφῷ ἐν Χριστῷ
Χαίρε

Βασιλέα τῇ κη Δεκεμβρίου 1772

Non possum comprehendere quare non misisti Biblia sacra in Basilea, sicut tua promessione. σὺ ἀγαπητὲ δέδωκες ἐξ ὅλης τῆς καρδίας, εἰς μνημόσυνον, καὶ νῦν οὐκ οἶδα αὐτήν. ἀκήκοα ἐκ στόματος τοῦ ἀδελφοῦ ἐν Χριστῷ, Κυρίου Brenner, ὅτι ἡ Χρυσημωτάτη Κυρία γυνή σου οὐκ ἔστιν βέλτιον, καὶ περίλυπος τῶν καρδίαν εὑρισκόμεθα. ἐλπίζω ὅτι ἡ λύπη σου εἰς χαρὰν ἐλθεῖν. σὺ γινώσκεις ἀγαπητὲ ὅτι ὁ γλυκύτατος Ἰησοῦς Χριστὸς, εἶναι ἡ ὁδὸς, ἡ ζωὴ καὶ ἡ ἀλήθεια, καὶ ὁ ἰατρὸς, καὶ οὐκ ἀφήσοι σε ὀρφανῷ. ἐγὼ πορευθήσομαι εἰς Μπέρνα, καὶ ἐὰν ἀγαπᾷς καὶ θέλεις ἀπὸ καρδίας ἵνα πέμψῃς μου τὴν παλαιὰν διαθήκην, εἰς Βασιλέαν, εἰς τὸν Κύριον Brenner, καλὸς ἔστι, εἰ δὲ καὶ οὐ θέλεις εὐχαριστῶ πάλιν σε ἀγαπῶ καὶ φιλῶ ἀπὸ καρδίας. ἀσπάζου τὴν κυρίαν γυνή σου ἐν φιλήματι ἀγάπης. τοῦτο ποιεῖ καὶ ἡ ἀδελφή μου. ἀσπάζου τοὺς φίλους καὶ τὴν ἐκκλησίαν τοῦ Χριστοῦ. ὁ Θεὸς τῆς ὑπομονῆς καὶ τῆς παρακλήσεως, δώσῃ σου ἵνα πάντα τὰ ἐρχόμενα τῷ ἀνθρώπῳ, εἴτε καλὰ εἴτε ἀγαθὰ, εἴτε κακὰ, ἵνα δοξάζῃς τὸν Θεὸν καὶ πατέρα τοῦ Κυρίου ἡμῶν Ἰησοῦ Χριστοῦ. ἔρρωσο.

ἐὰν ἀγαπᾷς γράψε ἐπιστολὴ εἰς Βέννα, ἵνα ἀκούσω τὰ περὶ τῆς Κυρίας

ὁ ἀδελφὸς ἐν Χριστῷ
Γεράσιμος Αὐλωνίτης ἐπίσκοπος

Letter of Gerasimos Avlonites to Johann Kaspar Lavater, December 28, 1772

TRANSLATION

To the Reverend Sir, Lord Deacon
and Brother in Christ,
Greeting.

Basel, the 28th of December, 1772

[Latin] I cannot understand why you have not sent the Holy Bible to Basel according to your promise. [Greek] You, beloved, promised from the whole heart, as I recall, and as yet I do not see it. I hear from the mouth of our brother in Christ, Mr. Brenner, that the excellent lady your wife is better, and the great grief of our hearts has been [discovered?]. I hope that your grief has changed into joy. You know, beloved, that our sweet Jesus Christ, who is "the way, the life, and the truth"[1] is also the healer, and will not leave one as an orphan.[2] I am going to Bern, and if you would like and want to send the Old Testament to Basel, to Mr. Brenner, it is good, but if you do not want to, I give you thanks, and again I love and cherish you with all my heart. Greet the lady your wife with the kiss of love, for she is also my sister. Greet the brothers and the church of Christ. The God of patience and comfort grant you all things for a human being, whether beautiful, or good, or evil, that you may praise the God and Father of our Lord Jesus Christ. Be strong!

your brother in Christ,
Erasimos Avlonites bishop

If you love [me], write a letter to Bern that I may hear about your lady.

1 John 14:6.
2 John 14:18.

21 Letter of Gerasimos Avlonites to Johann Kaspar Lavater

January 4, 1773

Source: Central Library of Zurich manuscript 'FA Lav. Ms. 501.149'.

TRANSCRIPTION

Τῷ πιστῷ καὶ ἀγαπητῶ ἀδελφῶ
ἐν Χριστῶ
Χαίρειν.

ὀυ δύναμαι κατανοεῖν τὴν αἰτίαν περὶ τῆς παλεὰς διαθήκις διὰ τι οὐκ ἔπεμψες. συ ἀγαπητὲ, ἀπὸ καρδιάς, καὶ ἑκουσίως, καὶ θαύσεος δέδοκες μᾶλλον ἔγραψες τὸ ὄνομα σου, καὶ νῦν βλέπω ὅτι ἀμεταβάχες τὴν γνώμιν. [Vestibus?] sicut dicimus esse virtutem ac proinde habitum cuius finis est gloria Dei et proximi salus; ostendimus diabolum et homines mendaces, non esse veraces, licet aliquando. verum docant: quia neque ex habitu id faciunt, neque istum finem spectant. οὐκ ἐπιλανθάνω τὴν χάριν καὶ ἐυεργεσάν ἅπερ ἠποίησες ἐν ἐμοὶ τοῦ ξένη ἀπὸ τοῦ νόσου τοῦτου; ἀλλὰ ούτὲ ἐπιλανθάνω ἕος θανάτου τοῦτου ὕπερ [άπερ?] πεποιήκες. σὺ ἀγαπητέ παρρησίαν ὑποσχὸμενος ἳνα πέμψεις μη τὴν θείαν γραφὴν, καὶ τοῦτο εἶναι γεγραμμένω ἄνω; ὢσται ευχαριστῶ καὶ περὶ ἐυχαριστῶ καὶ ἀθάνατω μνήμιν ἔχω περὶ σου κύριε. ἡ ἀδελφὴ μου ἀσπάζεται ἐν φιλήματι ἀγάπης τὴν κυρίαν γυνή σου, καὶ ἐγὼ τοῦτω ποιῶ. ἀσπάζου τοὺς φίλους, ἀσπάζου τὴν ἐκκλησίαν τοῦ θεοῦ. καθὸς βλέπω οὐκ ἀγαπὰς ἵνα γράψοίς μη ἐπιστολὴ ἵνα ἀκούσω καὶ χαρῶ διὰ τὴν ὑγείαν τὴς κυρίας γύνή σου πός ἐυρισκημένος. ἐγὼ εἰς τὰς προσέυχας μου δεόμενος Κύριου Ἰησοὺ χριστὸ[ς] περὶ σου, καὶ περὶ τῆς κυρίας γυνή σου, μετὰ παντὸς τὴς οἰκίας σού. ταῦτα γράφω et Deum ex animo comprecor ut tibi tuoque coniugi feminae lectissimae et liberis adeoque toti domui et familia clementer benedicat. ἐρρώσο.

P. S. μάρτυρα ἐπικαλούμενος Ἰησοὺν Χριστὸν ὅτι μέγα λύπη δεδυκέριος ἐν τὴ καρδία και ἁγία γραφὴ, μᾶλλον τὴς ἀδελφοίς μου. ἐγὼ πορευόμενος εἰς τὰς οὐ [ού?] ἐτῆ παρόντος μηιοὺς διὰ τὴν γενέβρα ός ήλιου θέλω γράψοι ἵνα μανθάνω περὶ σου, κύριε.

ἀπὸ πέρνα εἰς τὰς δ. το˜ Ἰάννουαρίου, 1773

φίλος καὶ ἀδελφὸς
ἐν Χῶ
Erasmus Aulonita
Episcopus Arcadiae
Candiae

Τῷ πιστῷ καὶ ἀγαπητῷ ἀδελφῷ
ἐν Χριστῷ
χαίρειν.

οὐ δύναμαι κατανοεῖν τὴν αἰτίαν περὶ τῆς παλαιᾶς διαθήκης διατί οὐκ ἐπέμψες. σὺ ἀγαπητέ, ἀπὸ καρδίας, καὶ ἀληθῶς, καὶ θελήσεως δέδωκες, μᾶλλον ἔγραψες τὸ ὄνομά σου, καὶ νῦν βλέπω, ὅτι ἀμετάβαλες τὴν γνώμην.
Veritas cum dicimus esse virtutem ac proinde habitum, cujus finis est gloria Dei et proximi salus; ostendimus diabolum et homines mendaces, non esse veraces, licet aliquando verum dicant: quia neque ex habitu id faciunt, neque istum finem spectant. οὐκ ἐπιλανθάνω τὴν χάριν καὶ εὐεργεσίαν ἅπαξ ἐποίησες ἐν ἐμοὶ τοῦ ξένου ἀπὸ τοῦ κόσμου τούτου; ἀλλὰ οὔτε ἐπιλανθάνω ἕως θανάτου, τοῦτο ἅπαξ πεποίηκας. σὺ ἀγαπητὲ παρρησίαν ὑποσχόμενος ἵνα πέμψεις μου τὴν θείαν γραφήν, καὶ τοῦτο εἶναι γεγραμμένον ἄνω; ὥστε εὐχαριστῶ καὶ περὶ εὐχαριστῶ, καὶ ἀθάνατον μνήμην ἔχω παρὰ σοῦ Κύριε. Ἡ ἀδελφή μου ἀσπάζεται ἐν φιλήματι ἀγάπης τὴν κυρίαν γυνή σου, καὶ ἐγὼ τοῦτο ποιῶ. ἀσπάζου τοὺς φίλους, ἀσπάζου τὴν ἐκκλησίαν τοῦ θεοῦ. καθὼς βλέπω οὐκ ἀγαπᾷς ἵνα γράψεις μου ἐπιστολὴν ἵνα ἀκούσω καὶ χαρῶ, διὰ τὴν ὑγίαν τῆς κυρίας γυναικός σου πῶς εὑρισκόμενοι. ἐγὼ

Letter of Gerasimos Avlonites to Johann Kaspar Lavater, January 4, 1773

TRANSLATION

To the Faithful and Beloved Brother
in Christ, Greeting!

I cannot understand the reason concerning the Old Testament, why you have not sent it. You, beloved, from your heart, willingly and [illegible] promised, no, rather, you signed your own name, and now I see that you have changed your mind. [Latin] [illegible], as we say, is a strength, and in the same way a character whose end is the glory of God and the salvation [good?] of one's neighbor. We show that the devil and human beings are liars, untruthful, in the end. Let them speak the truth, for neither do they do so from habit, nor do they look to that end. I am not forgetting the gifts and the hospitality that you once showed me, which were foreign to this disease, but nor do I forget until I die what you once did. You, beloved, who love frankness, promised that you would send me the Holy Scriptures that were written from on high. So I give thanks and concerning this; I have an undying memory concerning you, sir. My sister greets the lady your wife with the kiss of love, and I do the same. Greet the friends, greet the church of God. As I see it, you do not want to send me a letter that I may hear and rejoice about the health the lady your wife, how she is doing. I am keeping my prayers to Jesus Christ for you and the lady your wife, with all of your household. These things I write [Latin] and I pray God from the heart that he will bless you and the most learned lady your wife and your children and all of your household and family. [Greek] Be strong!

P.S. [Greek] I have called upon Jesus Christ as witness to that great grief that has appeared in my heart and [???] the Holy Scriptures more than that of my sister. I am coming in May [?] of the next year through Geneva [???]. I hope to write that I may stay with you, sir.

From Bern on the 4th of January, 1773

your friend and brother in Christ,
Erasmus Aulonita
Bishop of Arcadia [and?] of Candia

22 Letter of Gerasimos Avlonites to Johann Kaspar Lavater

Undated

Source: Central Library of Zurich manuscript 'FA Lav. Ms. 501.150'.

TRANSCRIPTION

Χαίρε ἀδελφὲ ἀγπητὲ
ἐν Χριστῶ

Si velis mittas ad Domino Excellentissimo Consulem ubi nos fuimus, ut audimus qui disoluit serenissimus senatus. παρακαλῶ ποίησον τοῦτο, ἐπειδὴ σὺ γινώσκοις ὅτι οὐδένα ἐχὼ φίλον μόνος σὺ ἀδελφὲ. φοβούμενος ὅτι ἡ ἄρχοντες τὴς πολεος, οὐ θέλουσιν ἵνα γένουσιν φιλάνθρωπος ἐν τῆ ταλαιπωρία μου. Λιπὸν παραδίδω πάντα εἰς χείρας Θεοῦ, ἅπερ αὐτος γινώσκος ταῖς ταλαιπώριας μου, καὶ ἀνάγκοι, καὶ πτωχοία. ἐρρωσο.

φίλος καὶ ἀδελφὸς
Ἐράσιμος ἐπίσκοπος

Si tibi est notum resolutione
scribas ad me pro mea consolationem.

TRANSLATION

Greetings, Beloved Brother in Christ

[Latin] If you would, you may send to the Most Excellent Consul about where we are, for we have heard that the most serene senate has been dissolved. [Greek] I beg you to do this, since you know that I have no friend but you alone, brother. I fear that the leaders of the city do not want you to be kind in regard to my suffering. So I leave all things in the hands of God, who knows my suffering, my need, and my poverty. Be strong!

your friend and brother,
Erasimos Bishop

If you know of any resolution, write to me for my consolation.

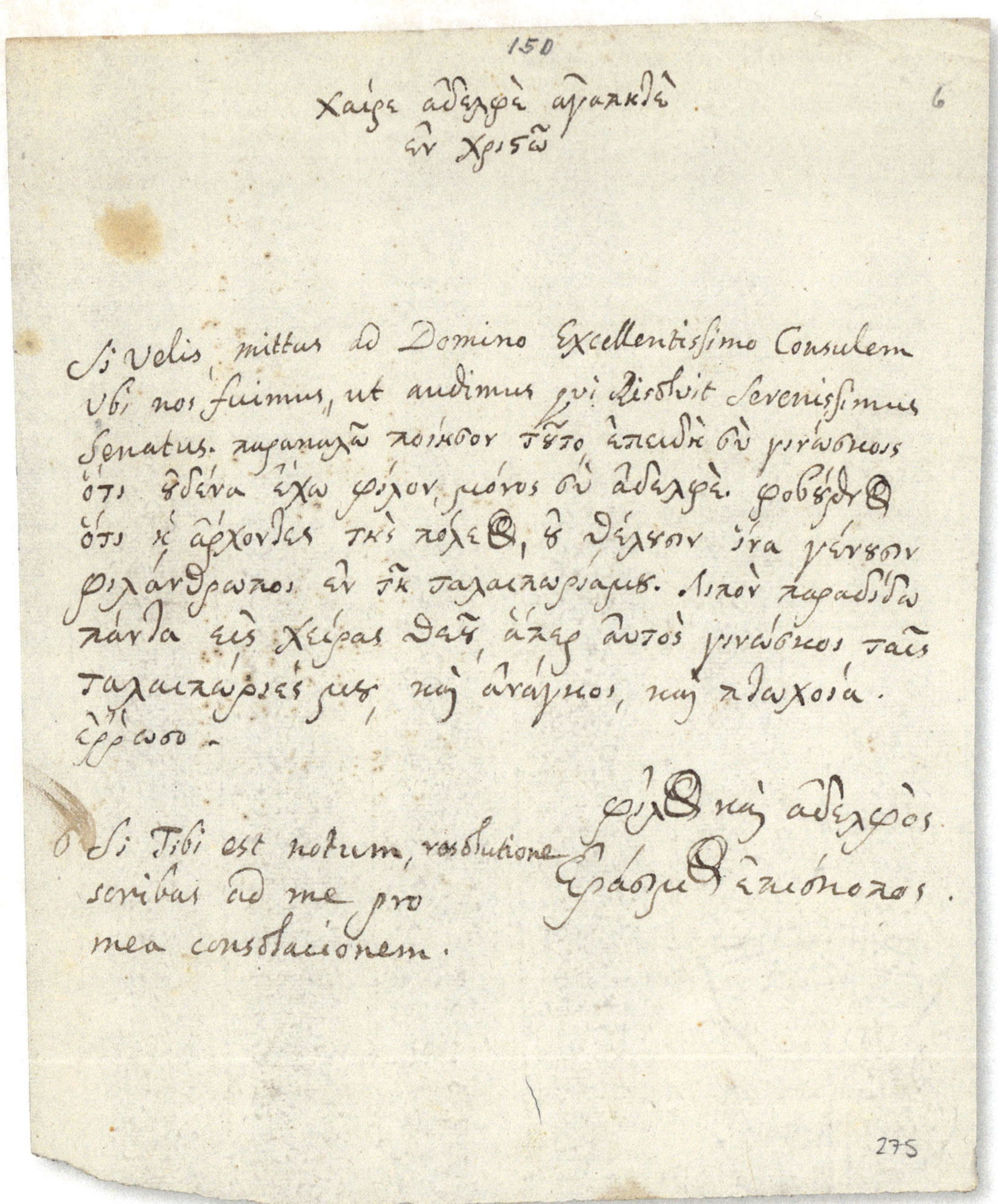

χαῖρε ἀδελφὲ ἀγαπητὲ ἐν Χριστῷ

Si velis mittas ad Domino Excellentissimo Consulem ubi nos fuimus, ut audimus qui dissolvit Serenissimus Senatus. παρακαλῶ ποίησον τοῦτο ἐπειδὴ σὺ γινώσκεις ὅτι οὐδένα ἔχω φίλον, μόνος σὺ ἀδελφέ. φοβοῦμαι ὅτι οἱ ἄρχοντες τῆς πόλεως, οὐ θέλουσιν ἵνα γένουσιν φιλάνθρωποι ἐν τῇ ταλαιπωρίᾳ μου. λοιπὸν παραδίδω πάντα εἰς χεῖρας θεοῦ, ἄπερ αὐτὸς γινώσκει ταῖς ταλαιπωρίες μου, καὶ ἀνάγκαις, καὶ πτωχεία. ἔρρωσο.

φίλος καὶ ἀδελφὸς
Γεράσιμος ἐπίσκοπος.

Si Tibi est notum, resolutione scribas ad me pro mea consolacionem.

Letter of Gerasimos Avlonites to Johann Kaspar Lavater, undated